A CLASSIC
COINCIDENCE

PABLO CASALS

BACH AND THE BLUES

ROBERT JOHNSON

WORDS & PICTURES
GARY KELLEY

ICE CUBE PRESS, LLC
NORTH LIBERTY, IOWA, USA

Bach and The Blues:
Pablo Casals and Robert Johnson

First Edition

Isbn 9781948509343

Library of Congress Control Number: 2021952702

Ice Cube Press, LLC (Est. 1991)
1180 Hauer Drive
North Liberty, Iowa 52317 USA
www.icecubepress.com |
steve@icecubepress.com

The paper used in this publication meets the minimum
requirements of the American National Standard
for Information Sciences—Permanence of Paper for
Printed Library Materials, ANSI Z39.48-1992.

Manufactured in Canada

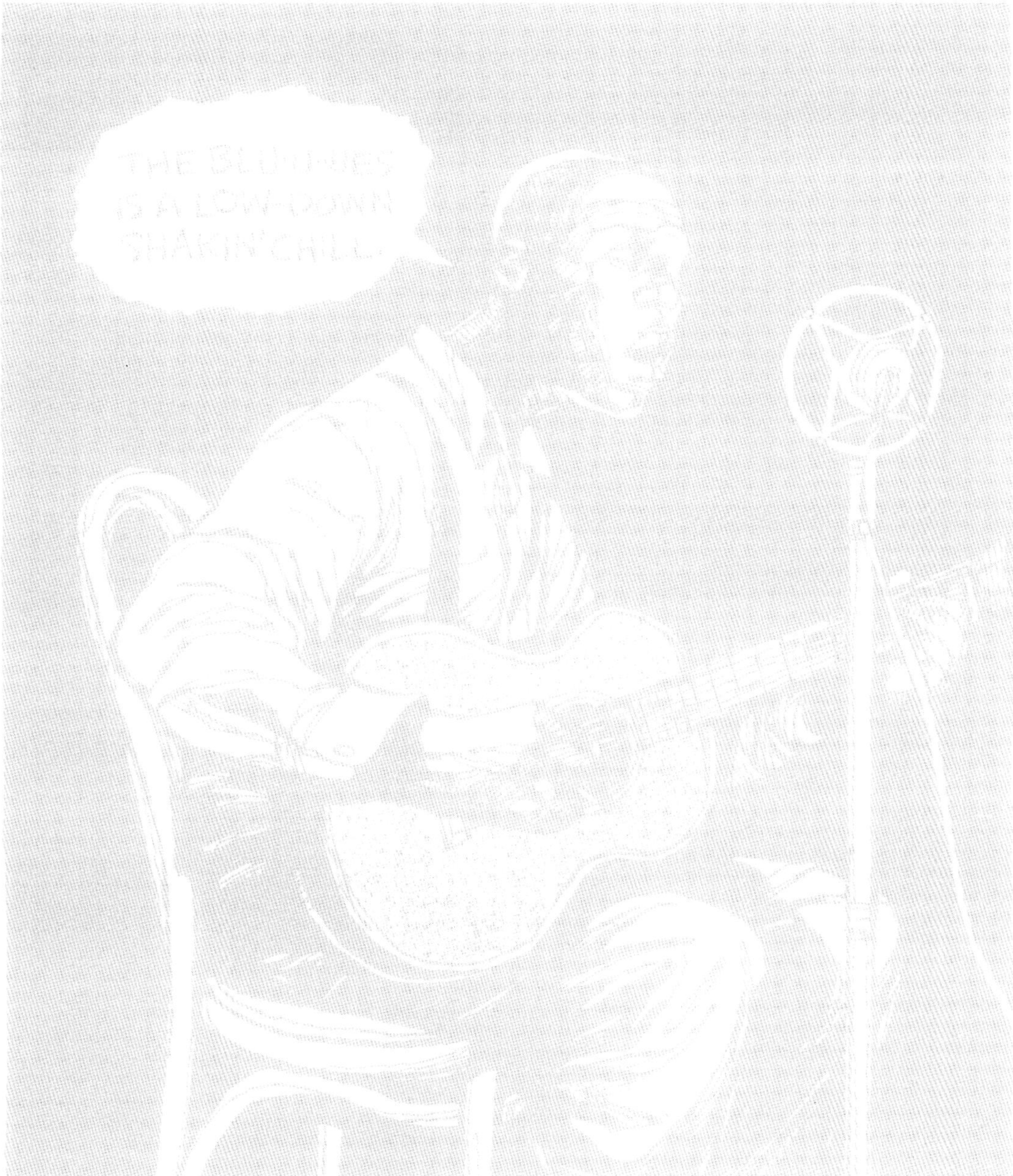
THE BLUUUES IS A LOW-DOWN SHAKIN' CHILL!

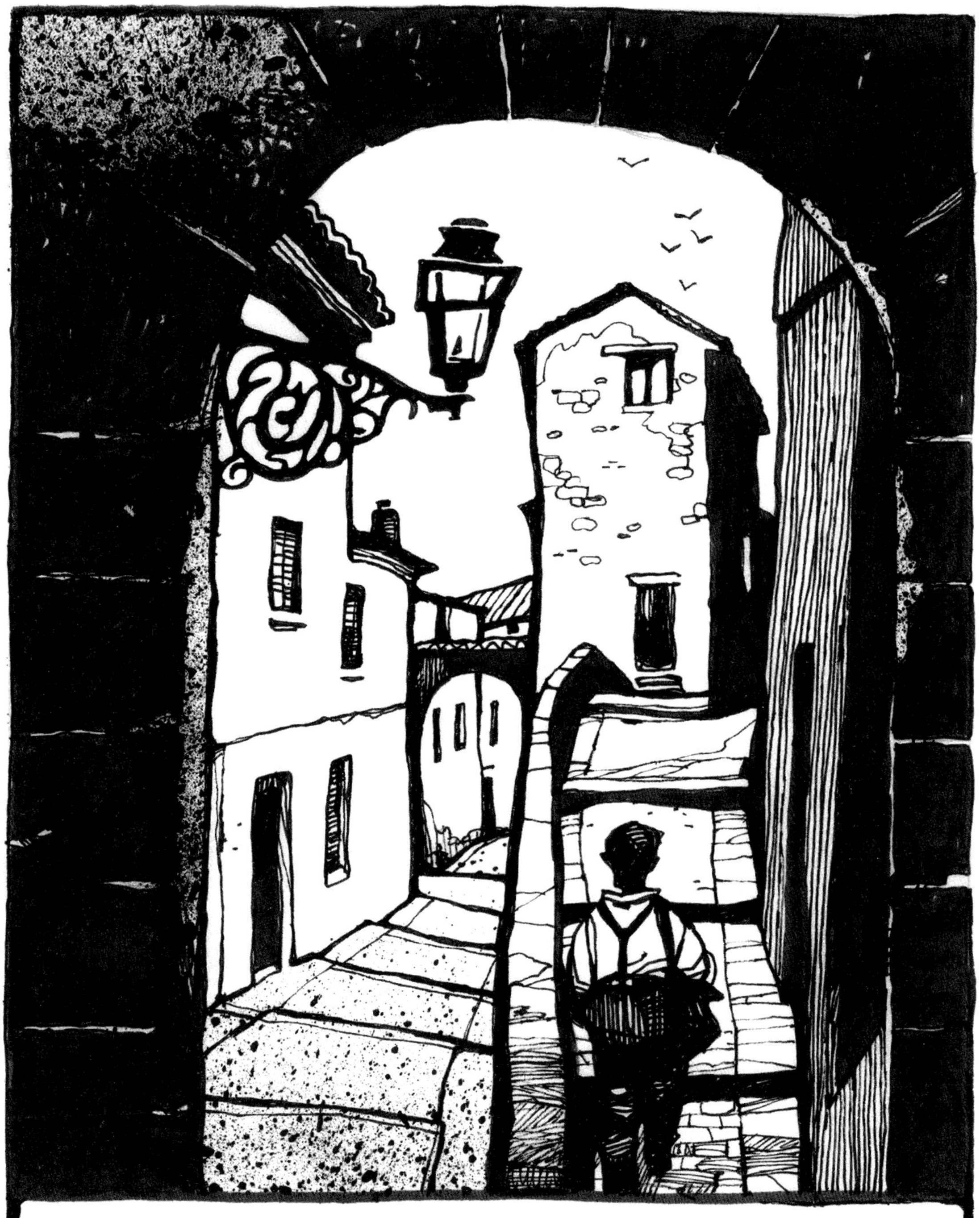
THE NORTHEAST CORNER OF THE IBERIAN PENINSULA ...A WEDGE BETWEEN THE PYRENEES MOUNTAINS AND THE MEDITERRANIAN SEA; SPAIN'S GREATEST REGION OF AUTONOMY AND INDEPENDENCE. ITS HEART... THE CITY OF BARCELONA, JUST UP THE COAST FROM THE VILLAGE OF VENDRELL... THE CHILDHOOD HOME OF FUTURE INTERNATIONAL CELLOMASTER PABLO CASALS.

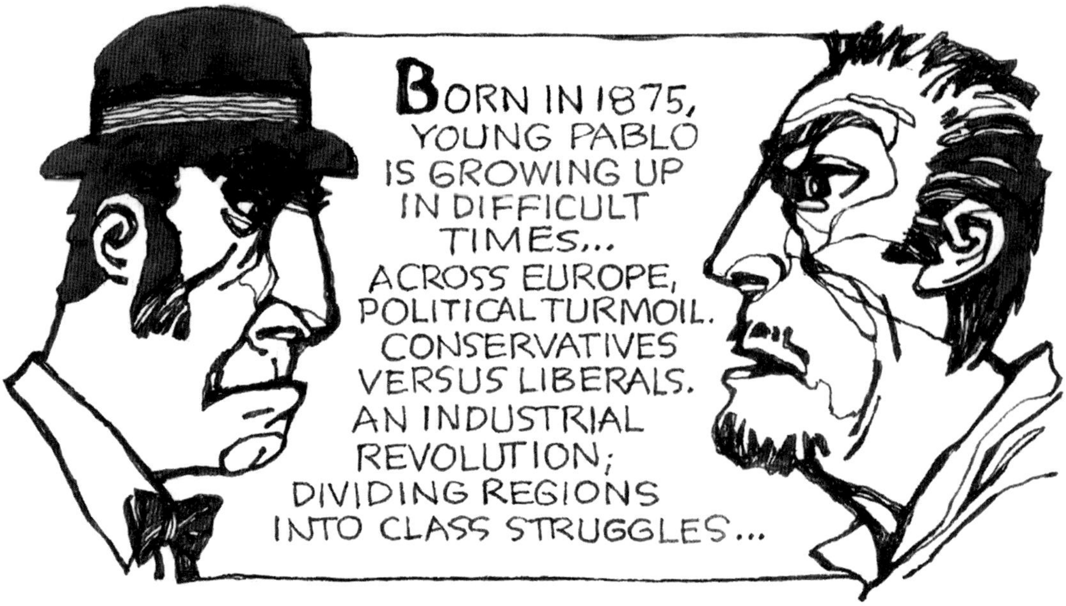
BORN IN 1875, YOUNG PABLO IS GROWING UP IN DIFFICULT TIMES... ACROSS EUROPE, POLITICAL TURMOIL. CONSERVATIVES VERSUS LIBERALS. AN INDUSTRIAL REVOLUTION; DIVIDING REGIONS INTO CLASS STRUGGLES...

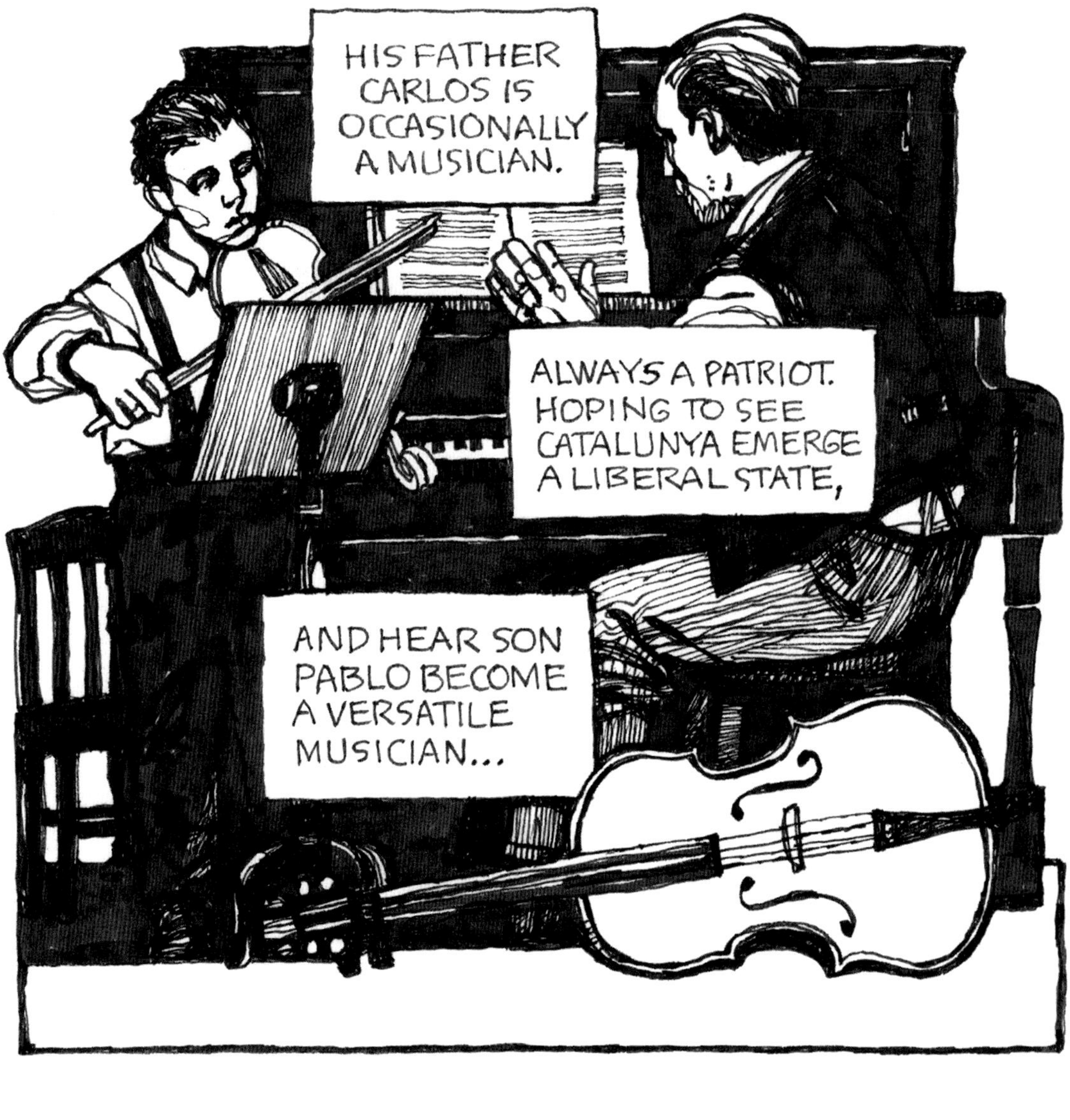
HIS FATHER CARLOS IS OCCASIONALLY A MUSICIAN.
ALWAYS A PATRIOT. HOPING TO SEE CATALUNYA EMERGE A LIBERAL STATE,
AND HEAR SON PABLO BECOME A VERSATILE MUSICIAN...

MOTHER PILAR ENCOURAGES SON PABLO TO PURSUE HIS PASSION.

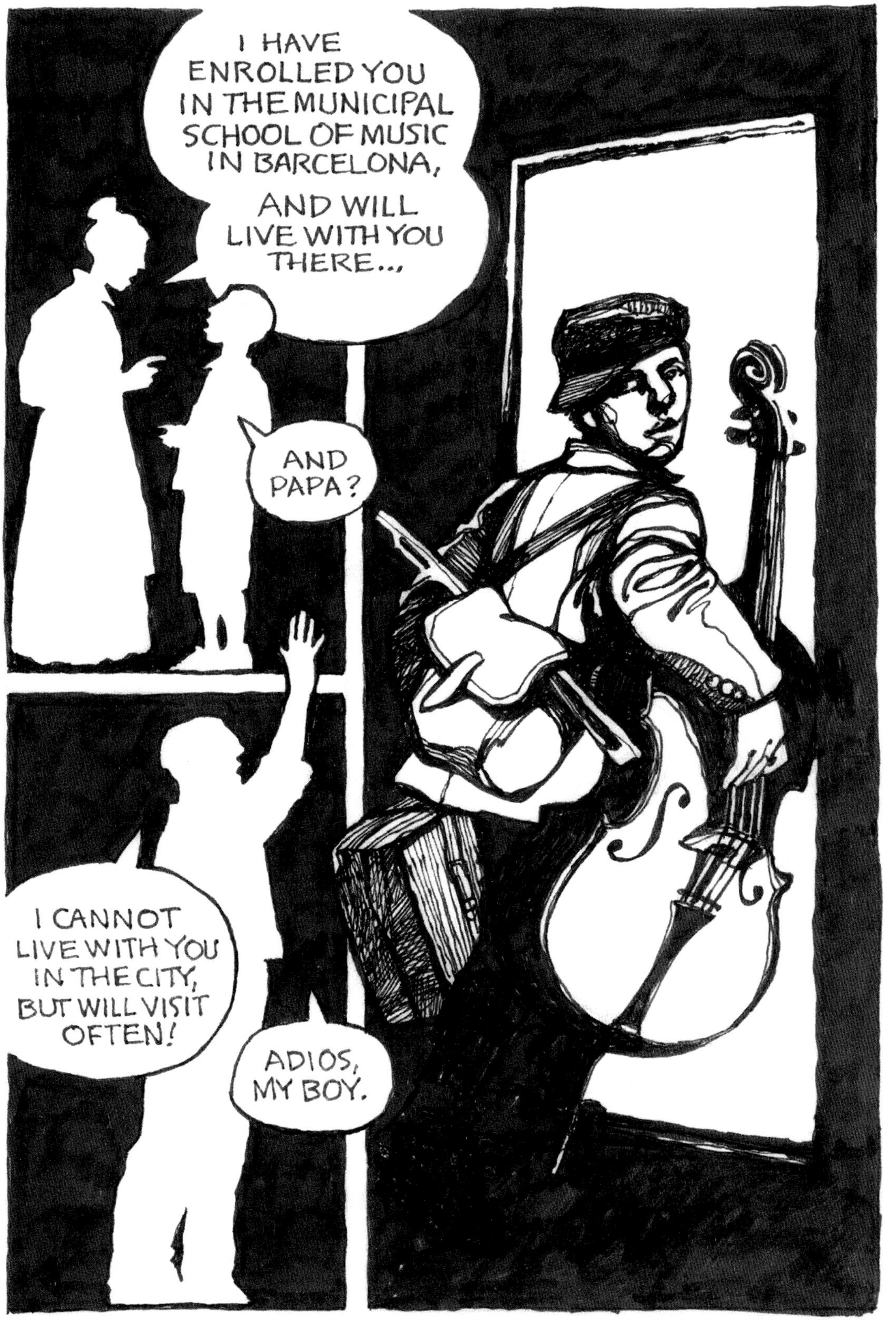
I HAVE ENROLLED YOU IN THE MUNICIPAL SCHOOL OF MUSIC IN BARCELONA,
AND WILL LIVE WITH YOU THERE...,
AND PAPA?
I CANNOT LIVE WITH YOU IN THE CITY, BUT WILL VISIT OFTEN!
ADIOS, MY BOY.

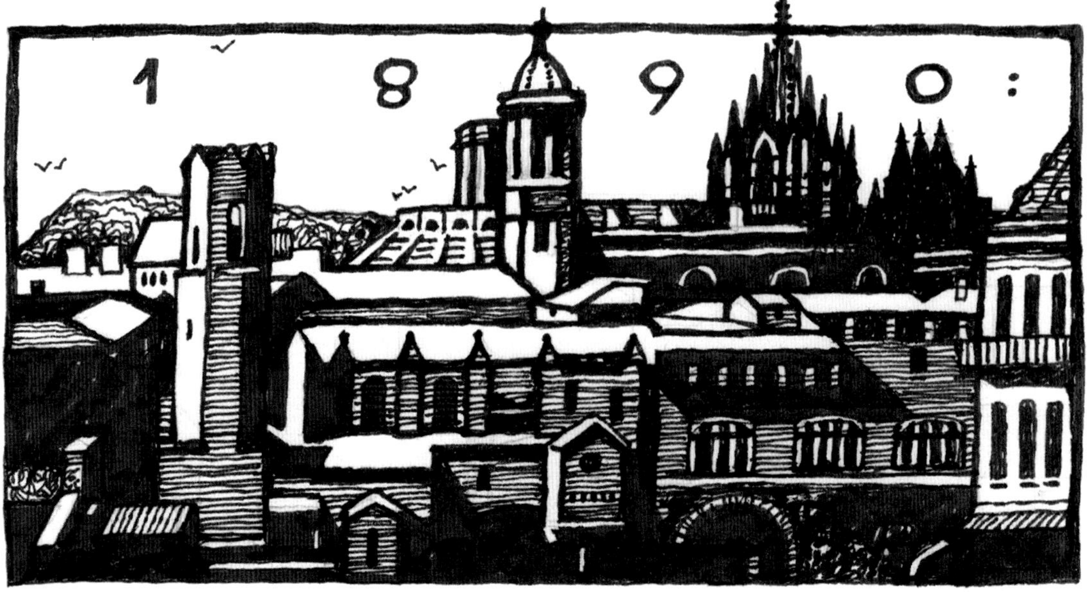
1890:

THANKS TO A LIVE-IN MOTHER, A WEEKEND FATHER, AND A POPULAR STUDENT TRIO PLAYING AT BARCELONA'S LIVELY *CAFE TOST* EVERY NIGHT OF THE WEEK...

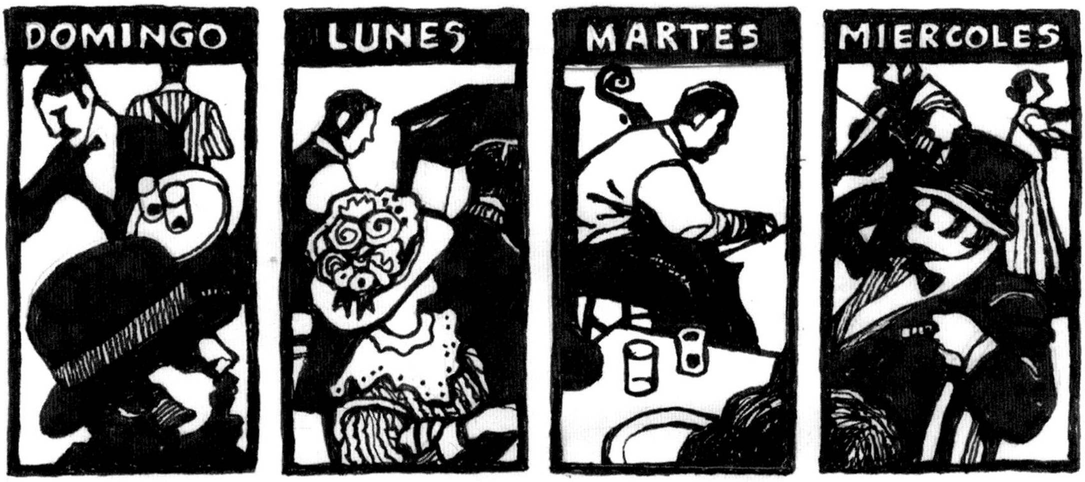
DOMINGO
LUNES
MARTES
MIERCOLES

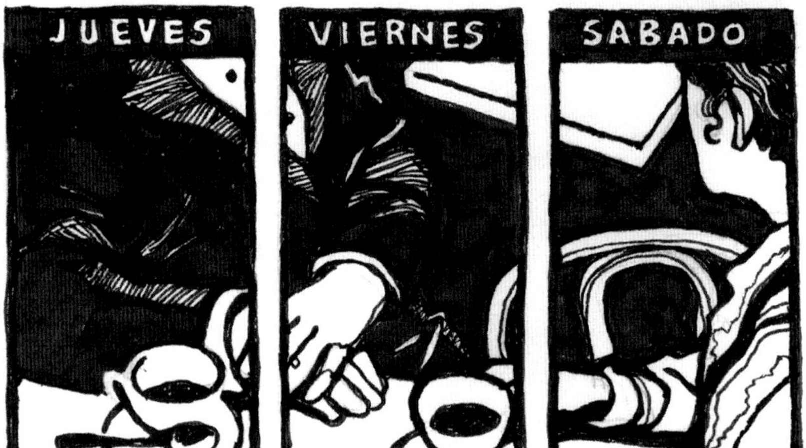
JUEVES
VIERNES
SABADO

...PABLO IS 'BLOOMING.'

CATALUNYA'S MODERNISMO METROPOLIS IS NOTICING. **EL NEN**...

'THE KID' WITH HIS CELLO.

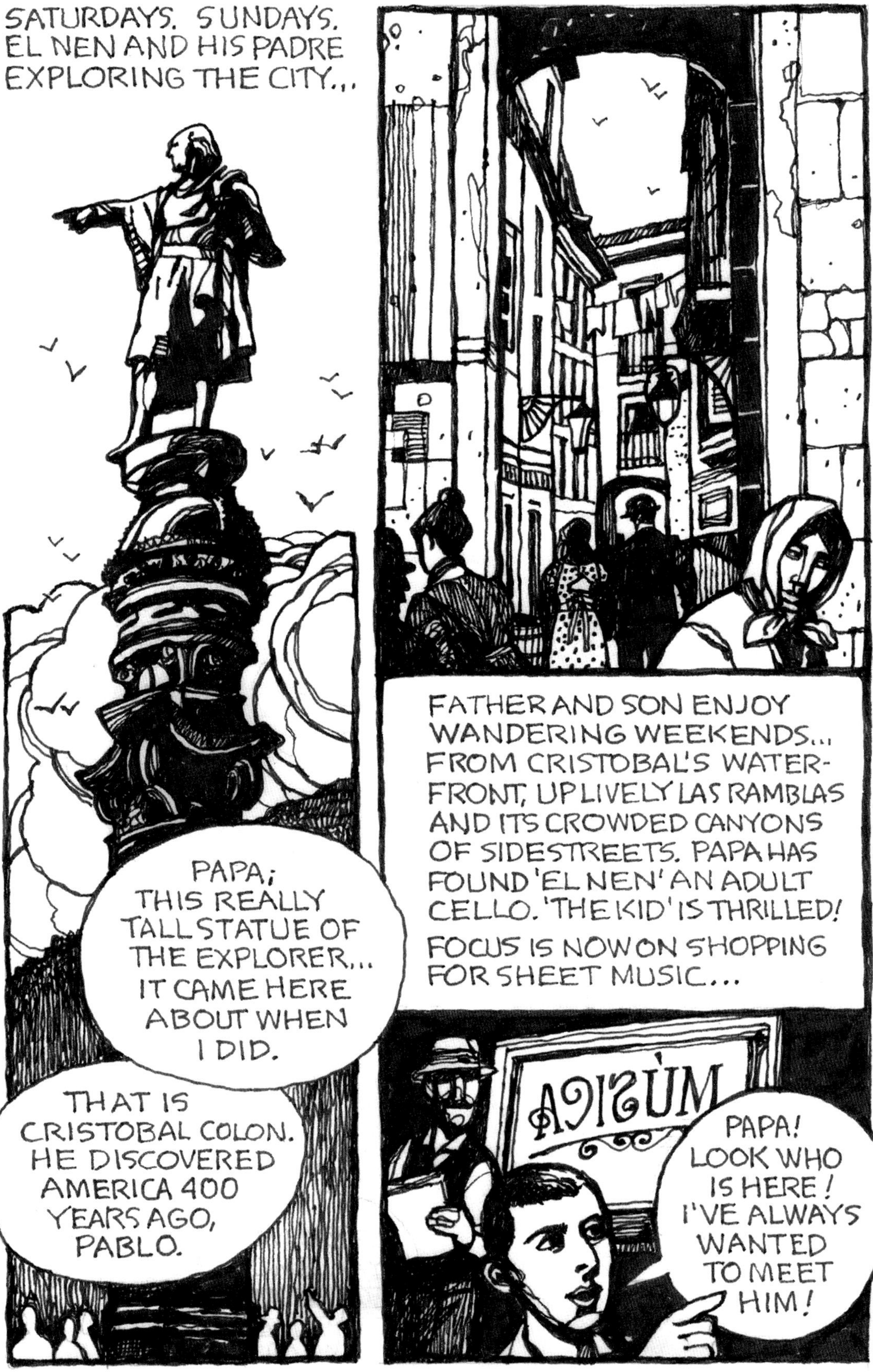
SATURDAYS. SUNDAYS. EL NEN AND HIS PADRE EXPLORING THE CITY...
PAPA; THIS REALLY TALL STATUE OF THE EXPLORER... IT CAME HERE ABOUT WHEN I DID.
THAT IS CRISTOBAL COLON. HE DISCOVERED AMERICA 400 YEARS AGO, PABLO.
FATHER AND SON ENJOY WANDERING WEEKENDS... FROM CRISTOBAL'S WATER-FRONT, UP LIVELY LAS RAMBLAS AND ITS CROWDED CANYONS OF SIDESTREETS. PAPA HAS FOUND 'EL NEN' AN ADULT CELLO. 'THE KID' IS THRILLED!
FOCUS IS NOW ON SHOPPING FOR SHEET MUSIC...
PAPA! LOOK WHO IS HERE! I'VE ALWAYS WANTED TO MEET HIM!

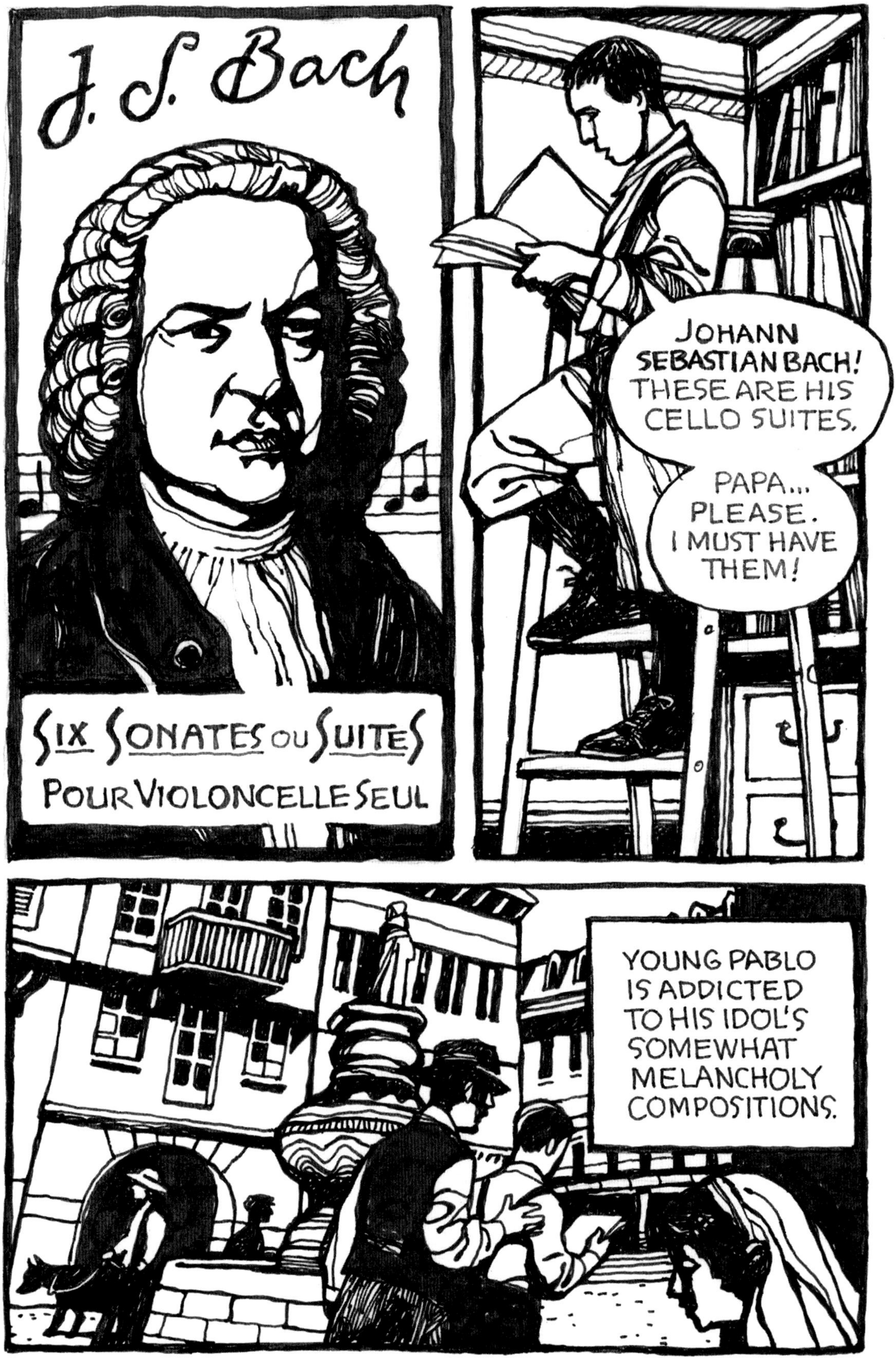

J. S. Bach
SIX SONATES OU SUITES
POUR VIOLONCELLE SEUL
JOHANN SEBASTIAN BACH! THESE ARE HIS CELLO SUITES.
PAPA... PLEASE. I MUST HAVE THEM!
YOUNG PABLO IS ADDICTED TO HIS IDOL'S SOMEWHAT MELANCHOLY COMPOSITIONS.

...SIX SUITES CRITICALLY REVIEWED AS (1) OPTIMISTIC, (2) TRAGIC, (3) HEROIC, (4) GRANDIOSE, (5) TEMPESTUOUS, AND (6) BUCOLIC. THE TEENAGER EMBRACES ALL.

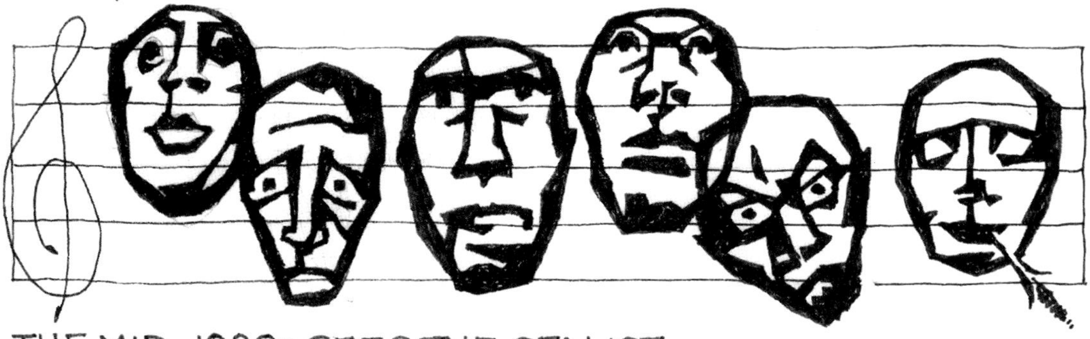

THE MID-1890s SEES THE CELLIST FINISHING SCHOOL IN BARCELONA AND ATTRACTING THE ATTENTION OF AREA MUSIC CRITICS.

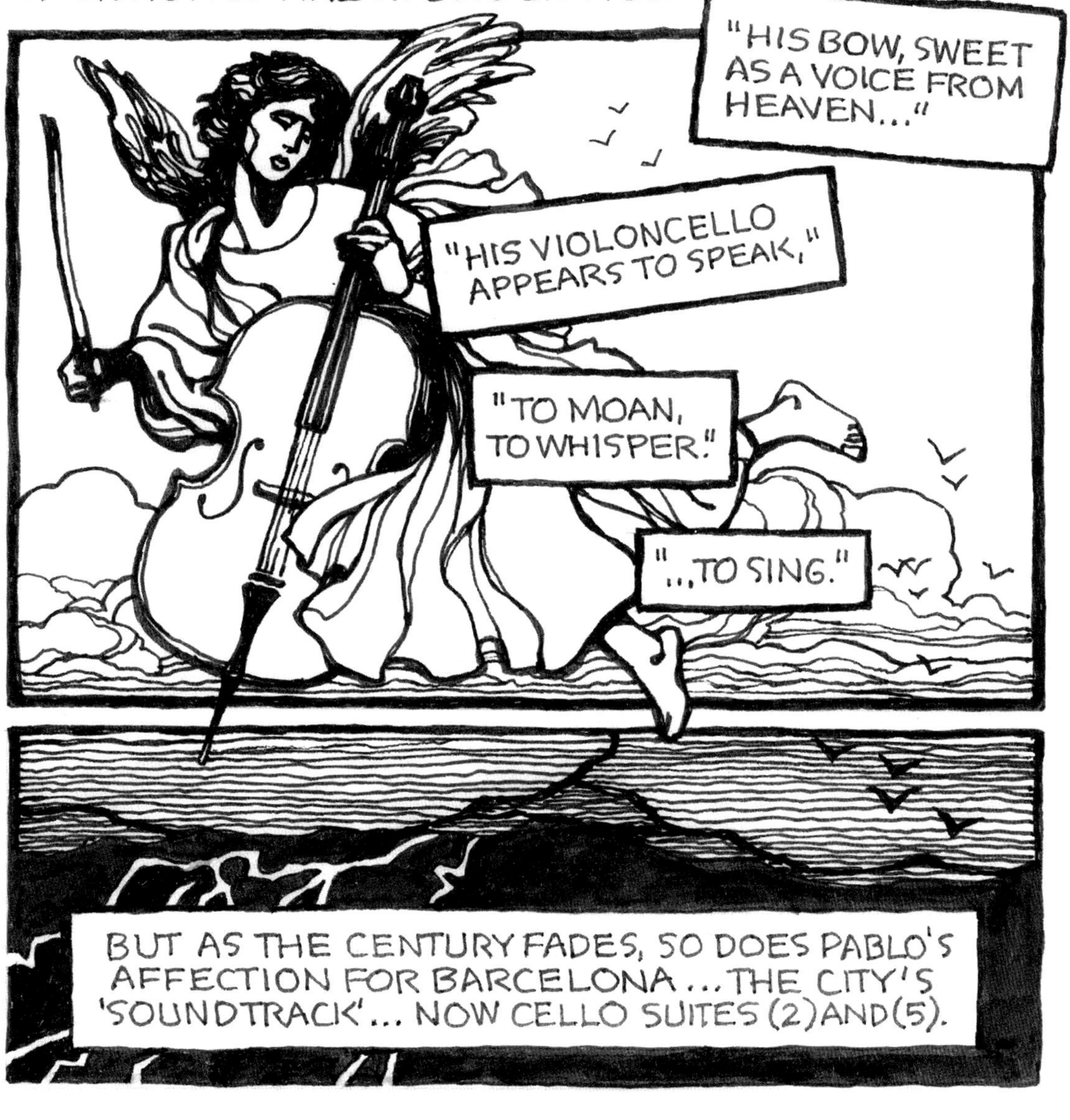
"HIS BOW, SWEET AS A VOICE FROM HEAVEN..."
"HIS VIOLONCELLO APPEARS TO SPEAK,"
"TO MOAN, TO WHISPER."
"...TO SING."
BUT AS THE CENTURY FADES, SO DOES PABLO'S AFFECTION FOR BARCELONA ... THE CITY'S 'SOUNDTRACK'... NOW CELLO SUITES (2) AND (5).

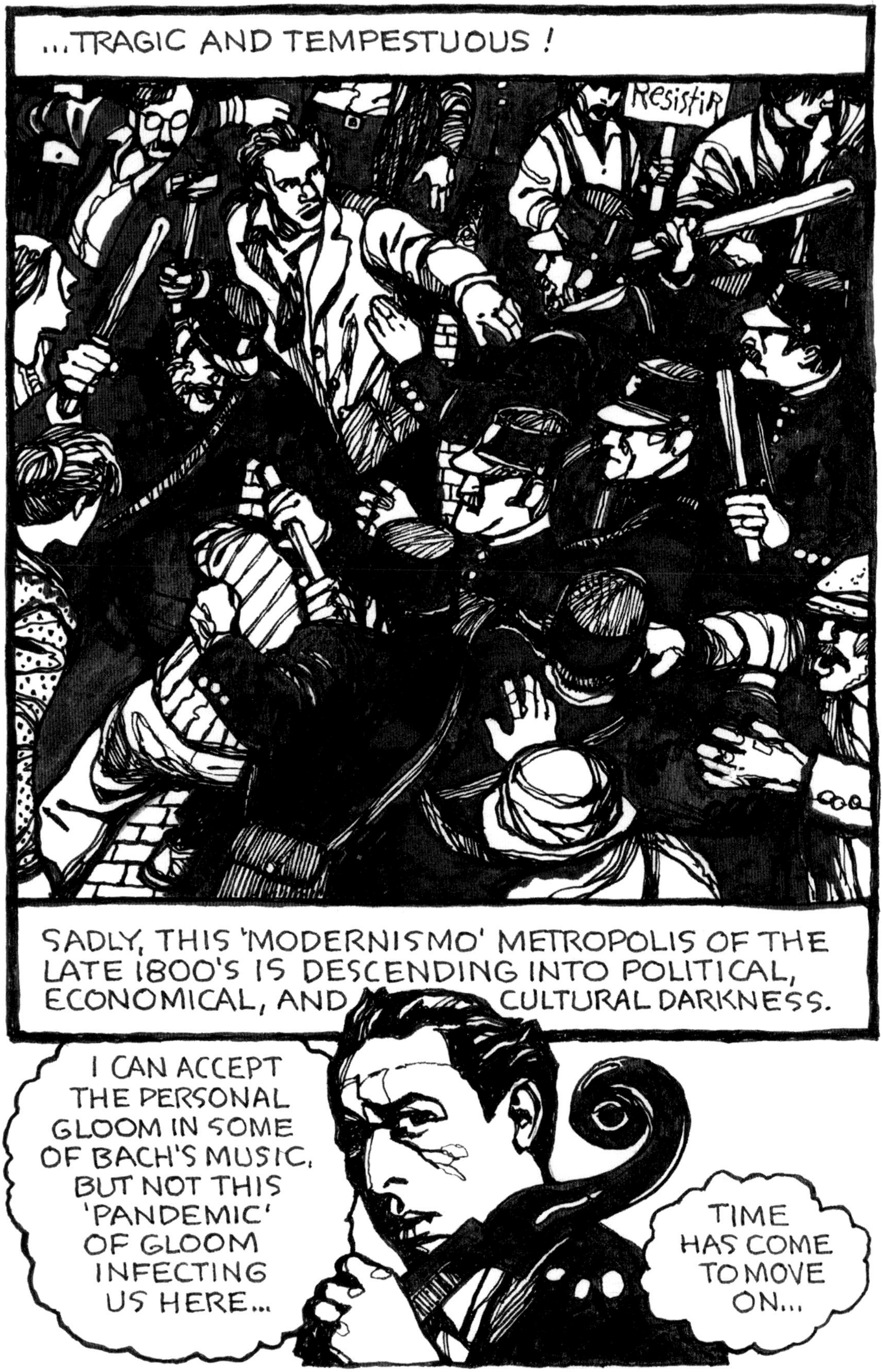
...TRAGIC AND TEMPESTUOUS !
Resistir
SADLY, THIS 'MODERNISMO' METROPOLIS OF THE LATE 1800'S IS DESCENDING INTO POLITICAL, ECONOMICAL, AND CULTURAL DARKNESS.
I CAN ACCEPT THE PERSONAL GLOOM IN SOME OF BACH'S MUSIC. BUT NOT THIS 'PANDEMIC' OF GLOOM INFECTING US HERE...
TIME HAS COME TO MOVE ON...

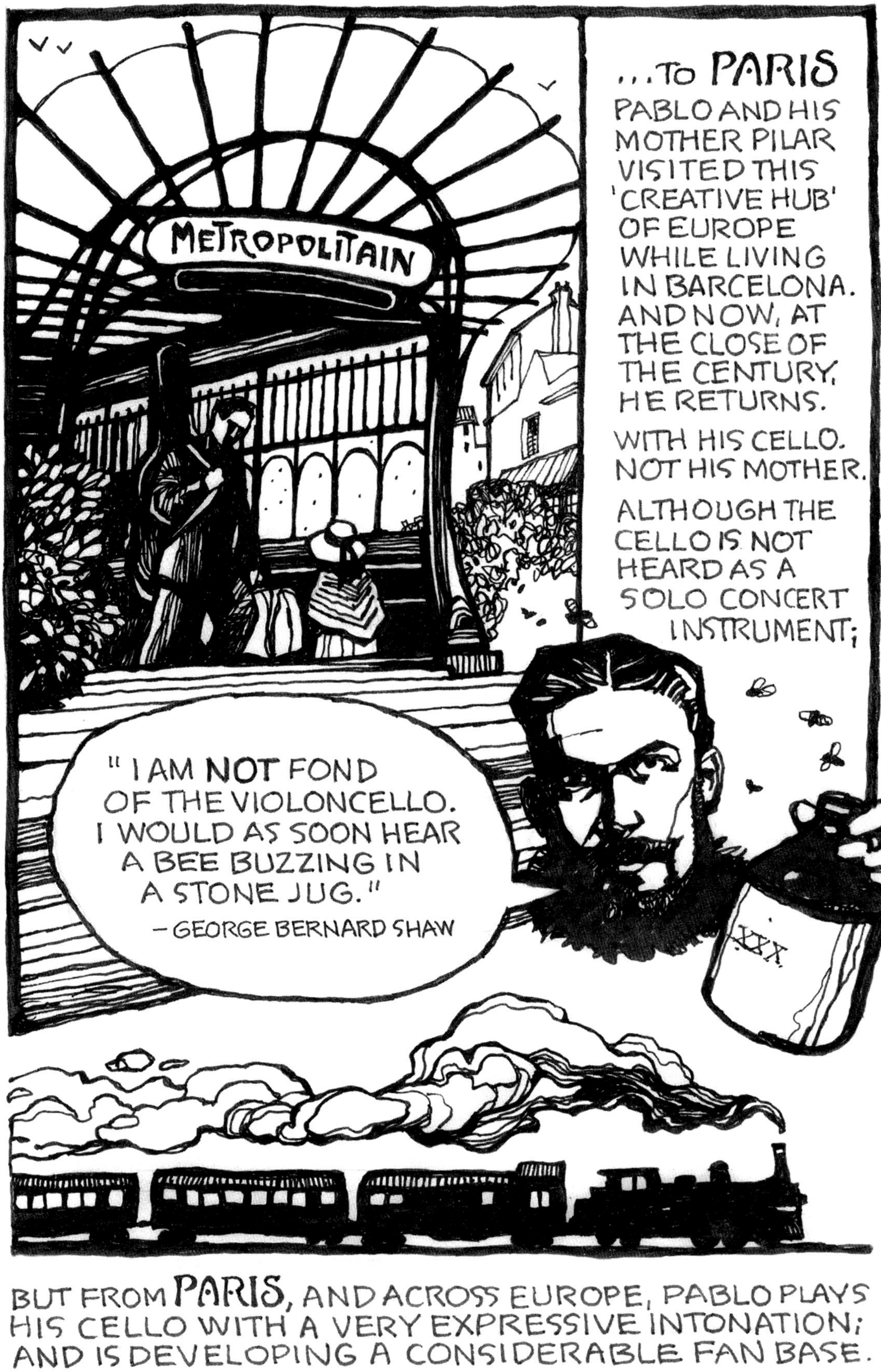
METROPOLITAIN
...TO PARIS
PABLO AND HIS MOTHER PILAR VISITED THIS 'CREATIVE HUB' OF EUROPE WHILE LIVING IN BARCELONA. AND NOW, AT THE CLOSE OF THE CENTURY, HE RETURNS.
WITH HIS CELLO. NOT HIS MOTHER.
ALTHOUGH THE CELLO IS NOT HEARD AS A SOLO CONCERT INSTRUMENT;
" I AM NOT FOND OF THE VIOLONCELLO. I WOULD AS SOON HEAR A BEE BUZZING IN A STONE JUG."
– GEORGE BERNARD SHAW
XXX

BUT FROM PARIS, AND ACROSS EUROPE, PABLO PLAYS HIS CELLO WITH A VERY EXPRESSIVE INTONATION; AND IS DEVELOPING A CONSIDERABLE FAN BASE.

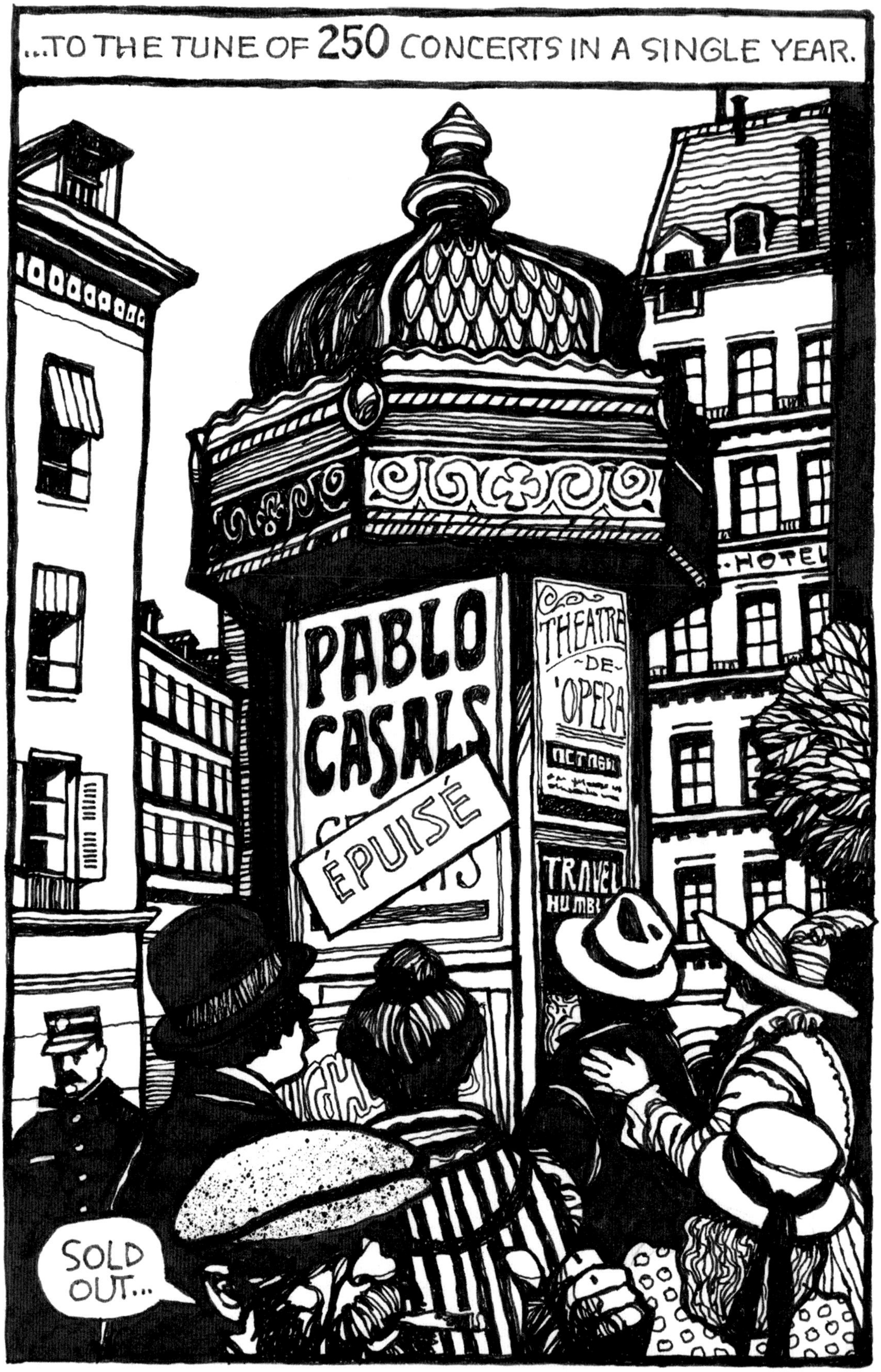
...TO THE TUNE OF 250 CONCERTS IN A SINGLE YEAR.
PABLO CASALS
ÉPUISÉ
THEATRE -DE- 'OPERA
TRAVEL
HOTEL
SOLD OUT...

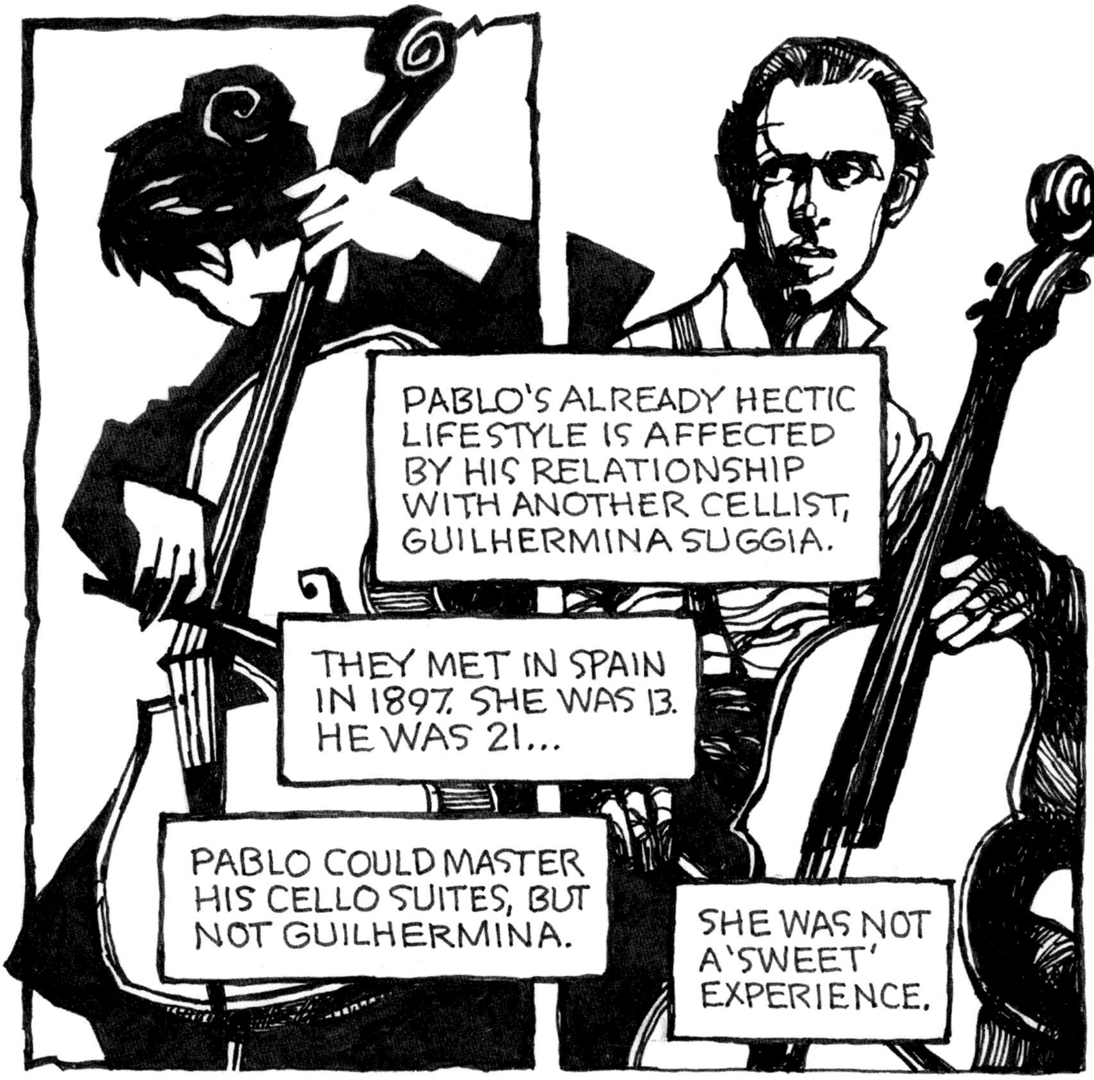
PABLO'S ALREADY HECTIC LIFESTYLE IS AFFECTED BY HIS RELATIONSHIP WITH ANOTHER CELLIST, GUILHERMINA SUGGIA.
THEY MET IN SPAIN IN 1897. SHE WAS 13. HE WAS 21...
PABLO COULD MASTER HIS CELLO SUITES, BUT NOT GUILHERMINA.
SHE WAS NOT A 'SWEET' EXPERIENCE.

ALTHOUGH A DECADE LATER, 1907, THE COUPLE IS STILL TOGETHER, IN PARIS, WHEN PABLO RECEIVES A SOMBER NOTE FROM HOME. A DEATH IN THE FAMILY. PAPA CARLOS. HE RETURNS TO CATALUNYA TO MOURN HIS FATHER... TO EMBRACE MOTHER PILAR AND HIS FAMILY.

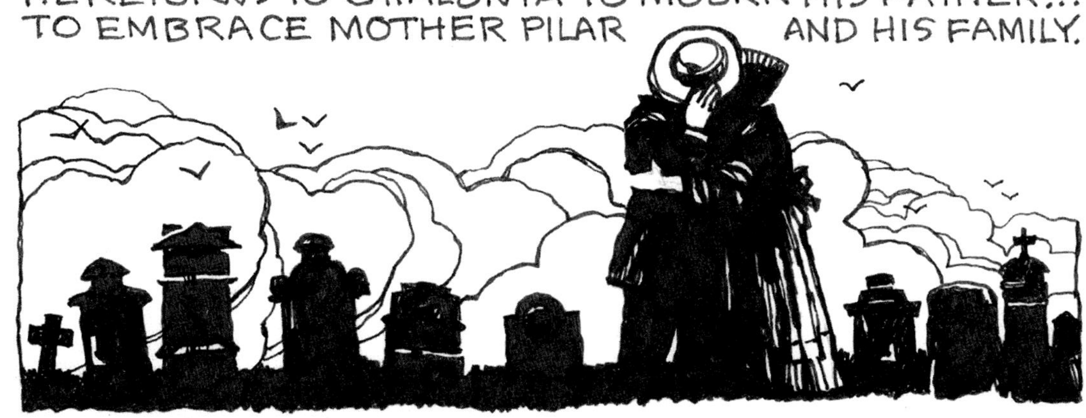

AND DISTANCE HIMSELF... FROM GUILHERMINA.

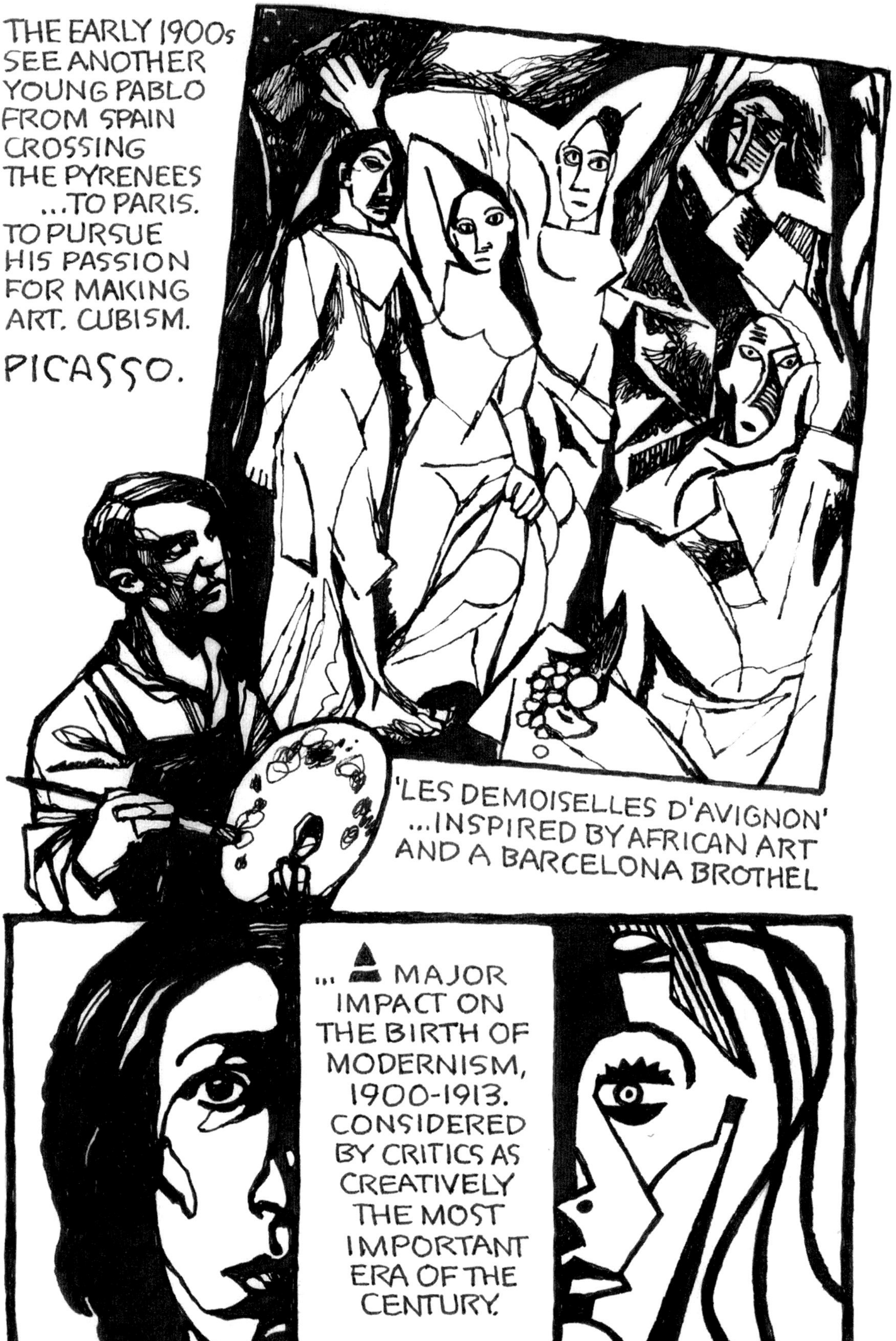
THE EARLY 1900s SEE ANOTHER YOUNG PABLO FROM SPAIN CROSSING THE PYRENEES ...TO PARIS.
TO PURSUE HIS PASSION FOR MAKING ART. CUBISM.
PICASSO.
'LES DEMOISELLES D'AVIGNON' ...INSPIRED BY AFRICAN ART AND A BARCELONA BROTHEL
... A MAJOR IMPACT ON THE BIRTH OF MODERNISM, 1900-1913. CONSIDERED BY CRITICS AS CREATIVELY THE MOST IMPORTANT ERA OF THE CENTURY.

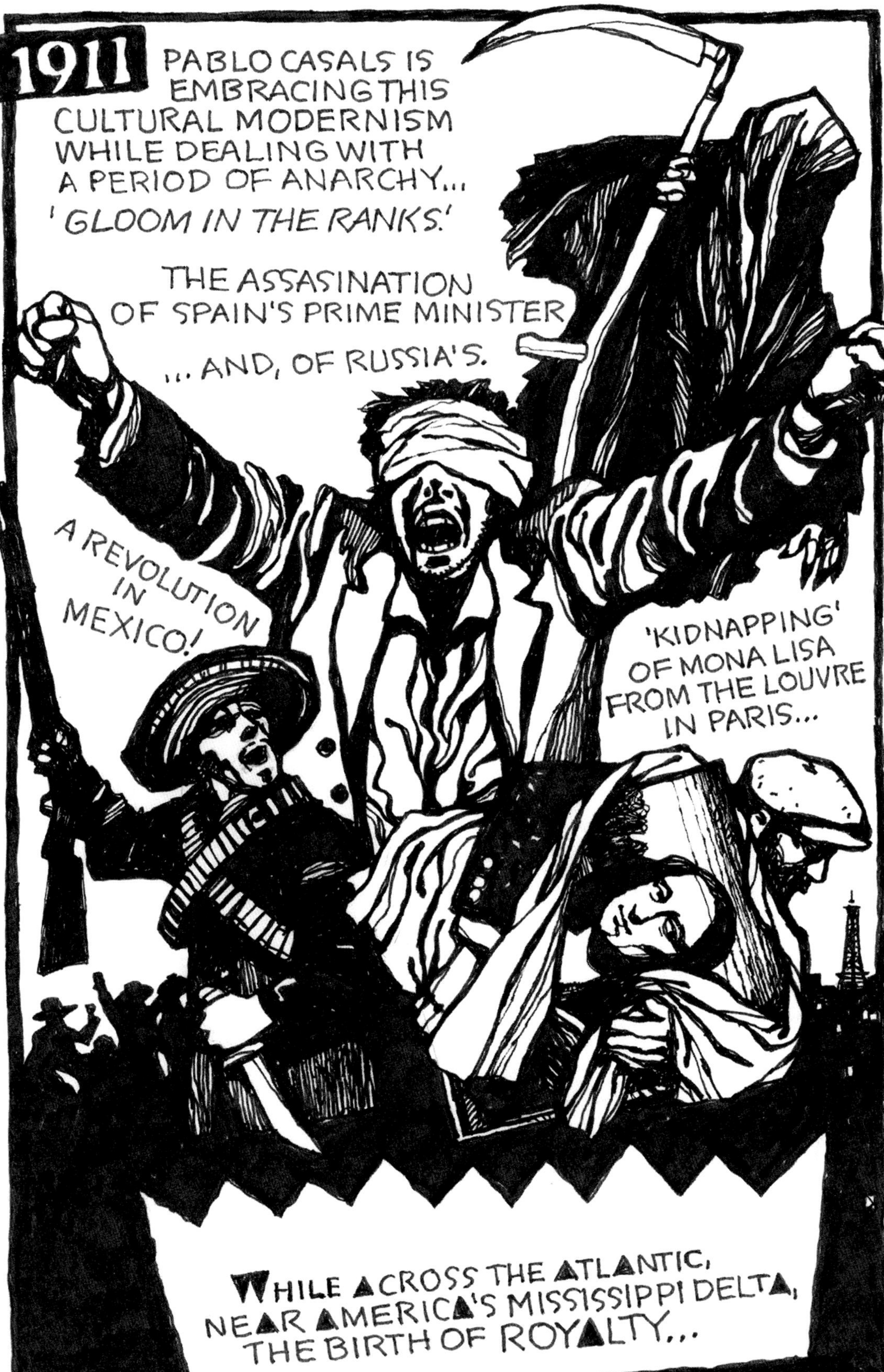

1911
PABLO CASALS IS EMBRACING THIS CULTURAL MODERNISM WHILE DEALING WITH A PERIOD OF ANARCHY...
'GLOOM IN THE RANKS.'
THE ASSASINATION OF SPAIN'S PRIME MINISTER
...AND, OF RUSSIA'S.
A REVOLUTION IN MEXICO!
'KIDNAPPING' OF MONA LISA FROM THE LOUVRE IN PARIS...
WHILE ACROSS THE ATLANTIC, NEAR AMERICA'S MISSISSIPPI DELTA, THE BIRTH OF ROYALTY...

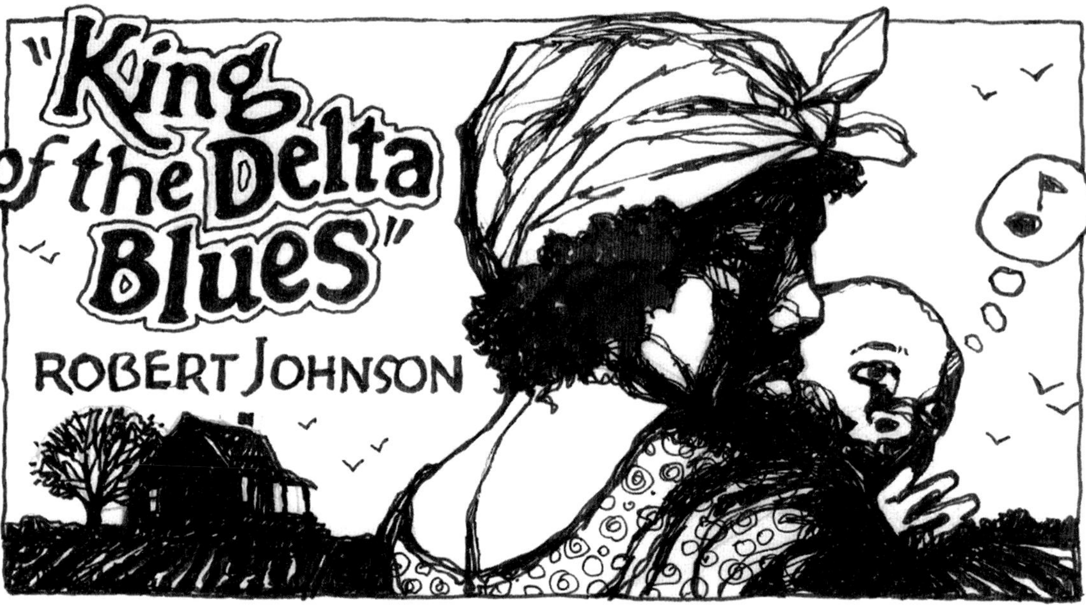
"King of the Delta Blues"
ROBERT JOHNSON

HE ARRIVES IN HAZLEHURST, MISSISSIPPI, 8 MAY 1911...

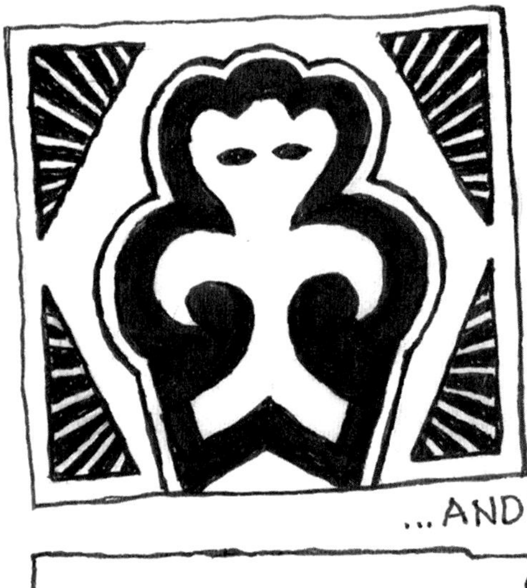

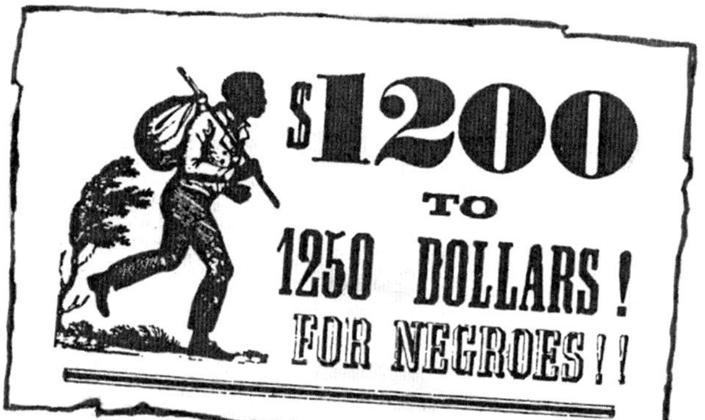
$1200
TO
1250 DOLLARS!
FOR NEGROES!!

HIS FAMILY TREE SPROUTED IN AFRICA.
...AND 'FERTILIZED' BY SLAVERY IN AMERICA.

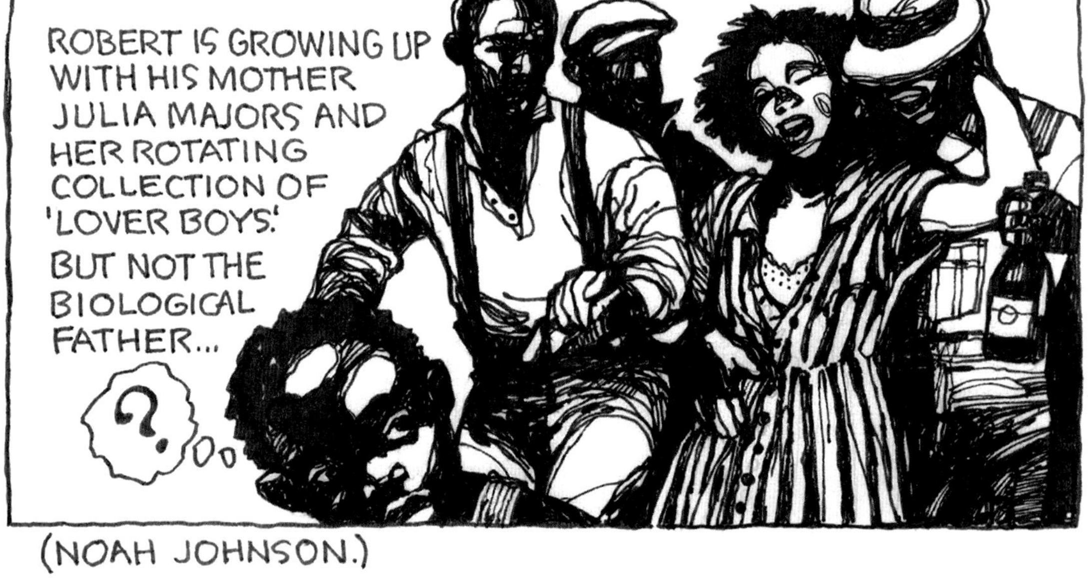
ROBERT IS GROWING UP WITH HIS MOTHER JULIA MAJORS AND HER ROTATING COLLECTION OF 'LOVER BOYS.'
BUT NOT THE BIOLOGICAL FATHER...
?

(NOAH JOHNSON.)

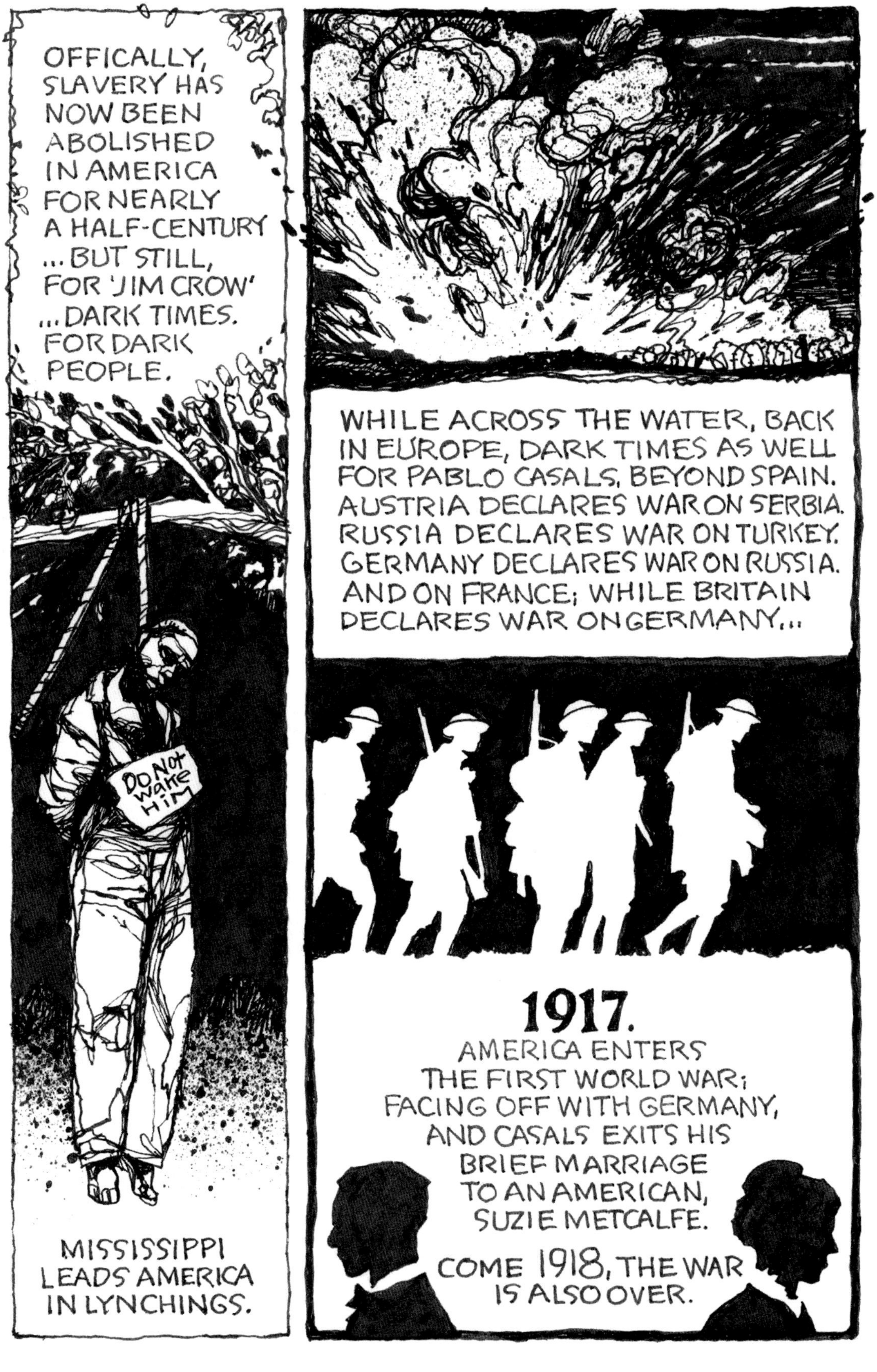
OFFICALLY, SLAVERY HAS NOW BEEN ABOLISHED IN AMERICA FOR NEARLY A HALF-CENTURY ... BUT STILL, FOR 'JIM CROW' ... DARK TIMES. FOR DARK PEOPLE.
DO NOT WAKE HIM
MISSISSIPPI LEADS AMERICA IN LYNCHINGS.
WHILE ACROSS THE WATER, BACK IN EUROPE, DARK TIMES AS WELL FOR PABLO CASALS, BEYOND SPAIN. AUSTRIA DECLARES WAR ON SERBIA. RUSSIA DECLARES WAR ON TURKEY. GERMANY DECLARES WAR ON RUSSIA. AND ON FRANCE; WHILE BRITAIN DECLARES WAR ON GERMANY...
1917.
AMERICA ENTERS THE FIRST WORLD WAR; FACING OFF WITH GERMANY, AND CASALS EXITS HIS BRIEF MARRIAGE TO AN AMERICAN, SUZIE METCALFE.
COME 1918, THE WAR IS ALSO OVER.

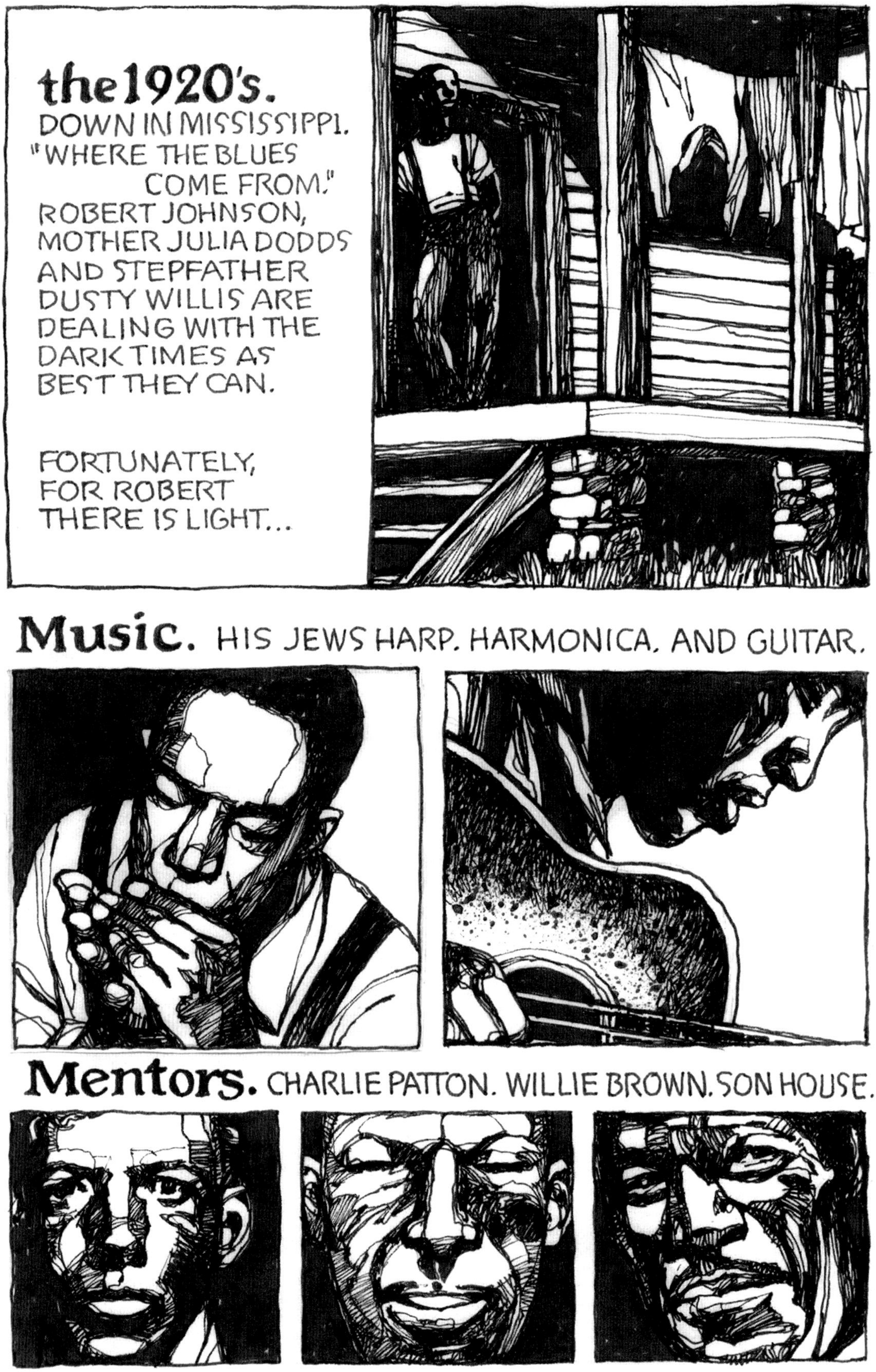
the 1920's.
DOWN IN MISSISSIPPI.
"WHERE THE BLUES COME FROM."
ROBERT JOHNSON, MOTHER JULIA DODDS AND STEPFATHER DUSTY WILLIS ARE DEALING WITH THE DARK TIMES AS BEST THEY CAN.
FORTUNATELY, FOR ROBERT THERE IS LIGHT...
Music. HIS JEWS HARP. HARMONICA. AND GUITAR.
Mentors. CHARLIE PATTON. WILLIE BROWN. SON HOUSE.

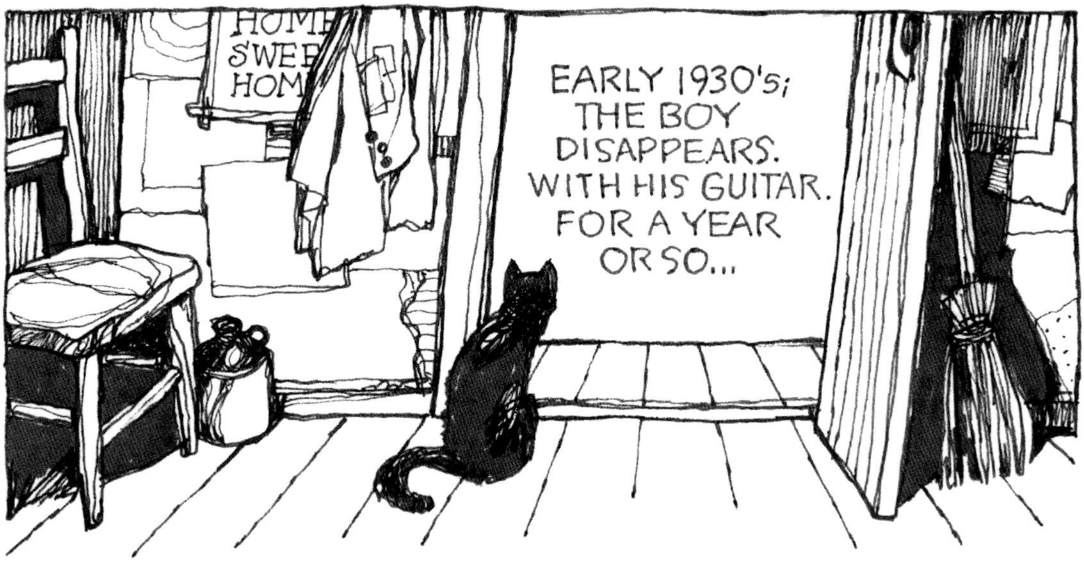
HOME SWEET HOME
EARLY 1930'S; THE BOY DISAPPEARS. WITH HIS GUITAR. FOR A YEAR OR SO...

AND RETURNS HOME, GROWING INTO A YOUNG LADIES' MAN. PLAYING GREAT GUITAR. AND PLAYING WITH WOMEN...

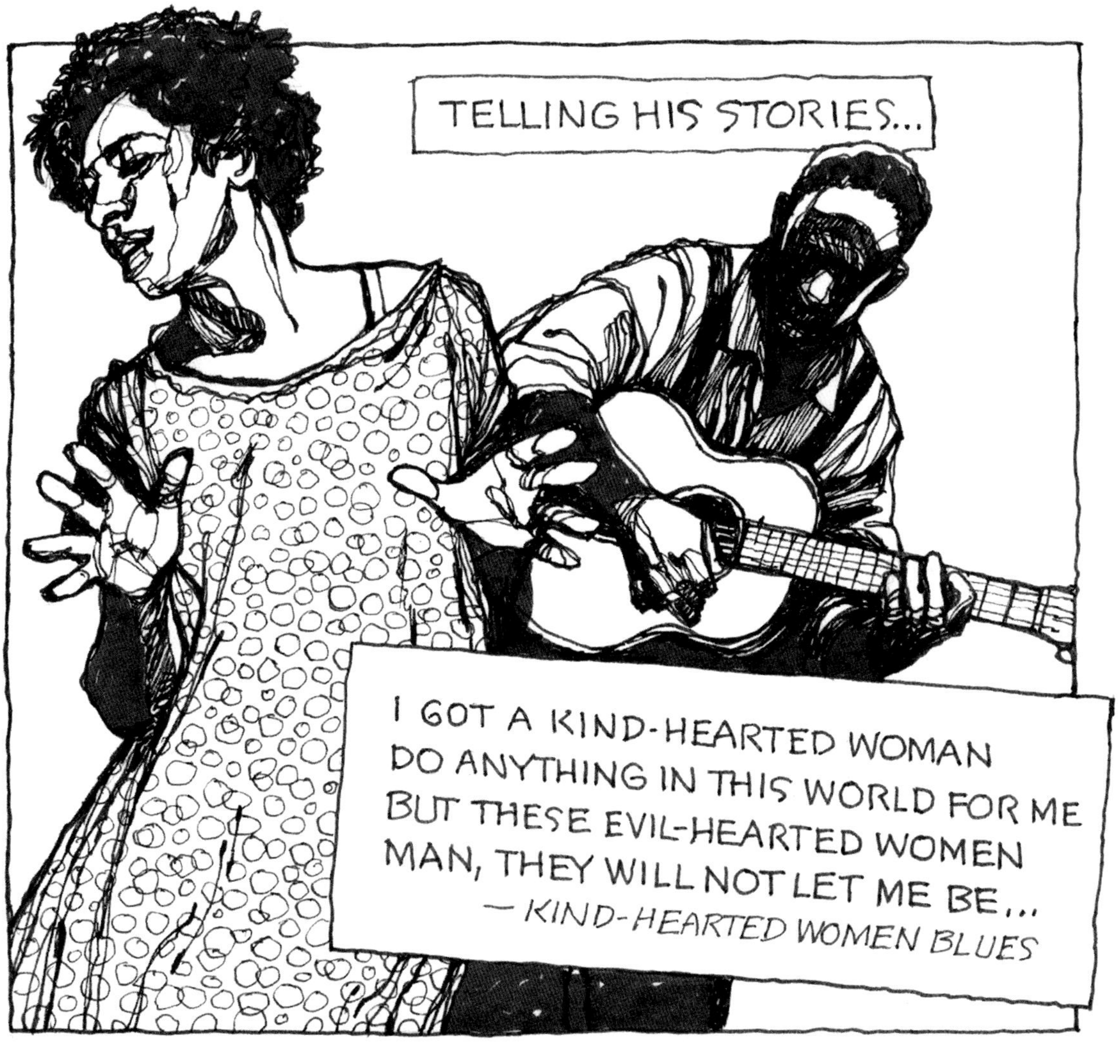
TELLING HIS STORIES...
I GOT A KIND-HEARTED WOMAN
DO ANYTHING IN THIS WORLD FOR ME
BUT THESE EVIL-HEARTED WOMEN
MAN, THEY WILL NOT LET ME BE...
— KIND-HEARTED WOMEN BLUES

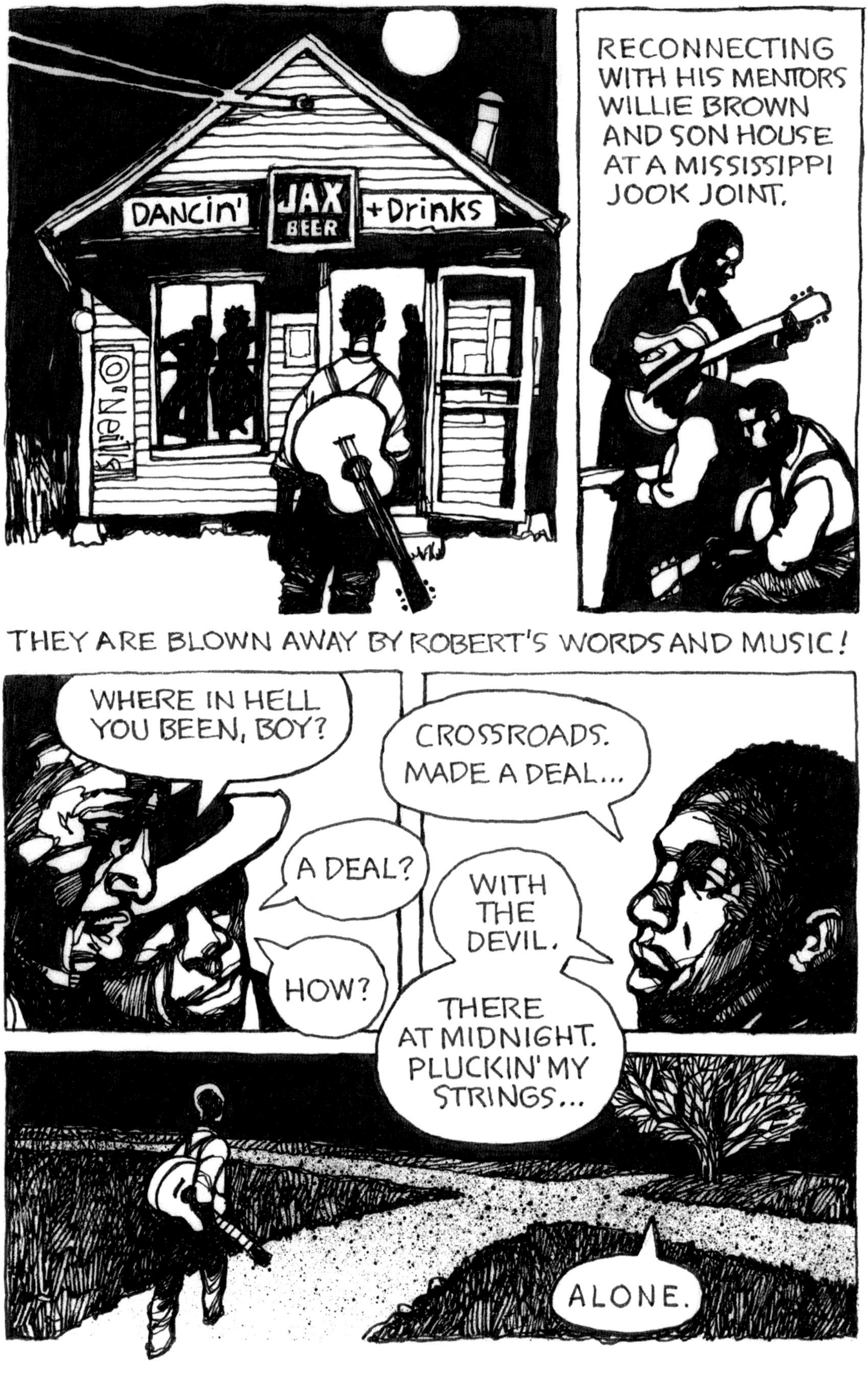
DANCIN'
JAX BEER
+ Drinks
RECONNECTING WITH HIS MENTORS WILLIE BROWN AND SON HOUSE AT A MISSISSIPPI JOOK JOINT.
THEY ARE BLOWN AWAY BY ROBERT'S WORDS AND MUSIC!
WHERE IN HELL YOU BEEN, BOY?
CROSSROADS. MADE A DEAL...
A DEAL?
WITH THE DEVIL.
HOW?
THERE AT MIDNIGHT. PLUCKIN' MY STRINGS...
ALONE.

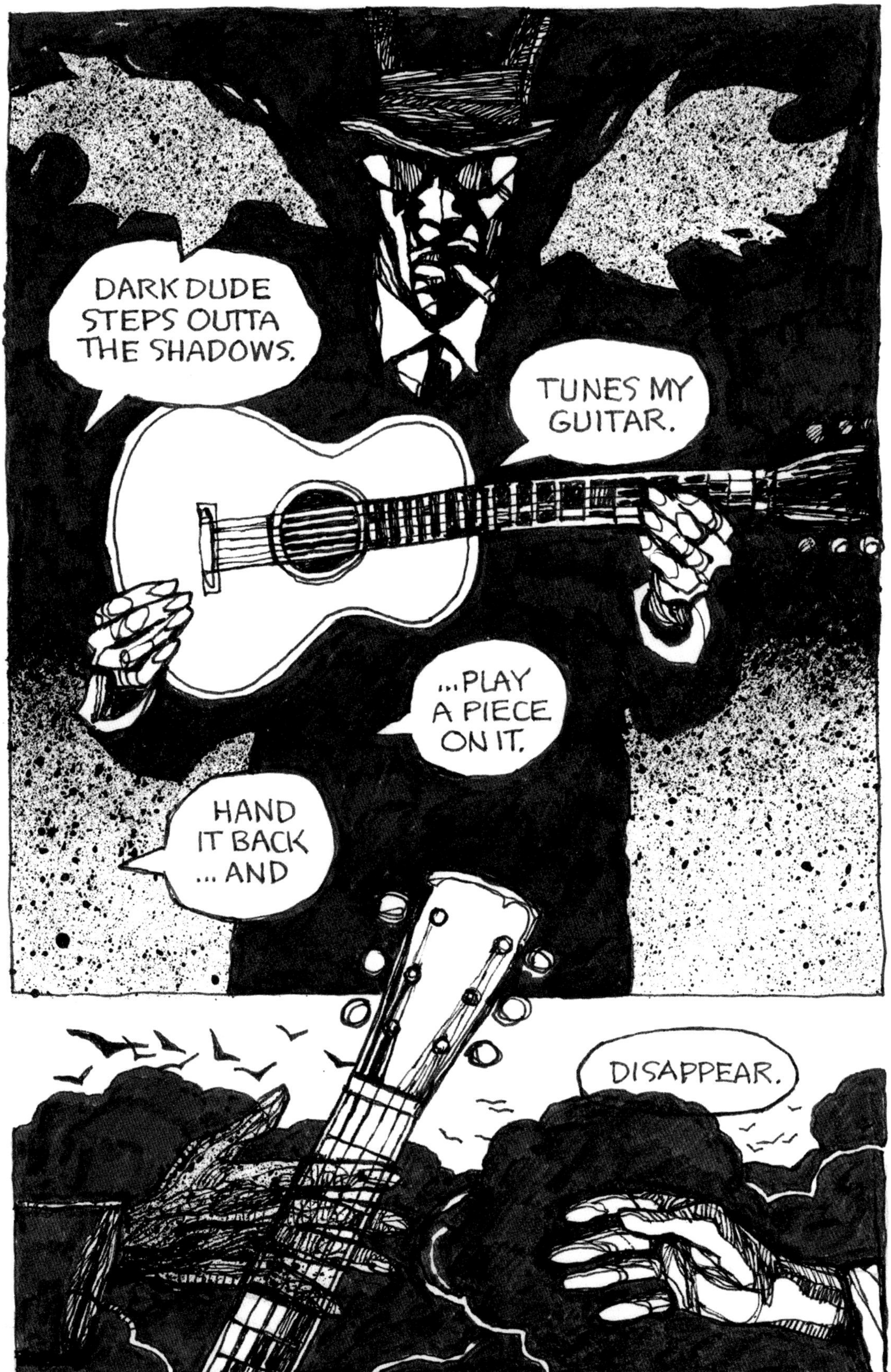
DARK DUDE STEPS OUTTA THE SHADOWS.
TUNES MY GUITAR.
...PLAY A PIECE ON IT.
HAND IT BACK ... AND
DISAPPEAR.

LEGEND HAS IT HIS MIDNIGHT MEETING AT THE CROSSROADS WAS THE SPARK THAT IGNITED ROBERT JOHNSON'S BRIEF CAREER. AND HIS EVERLASTING FAME.

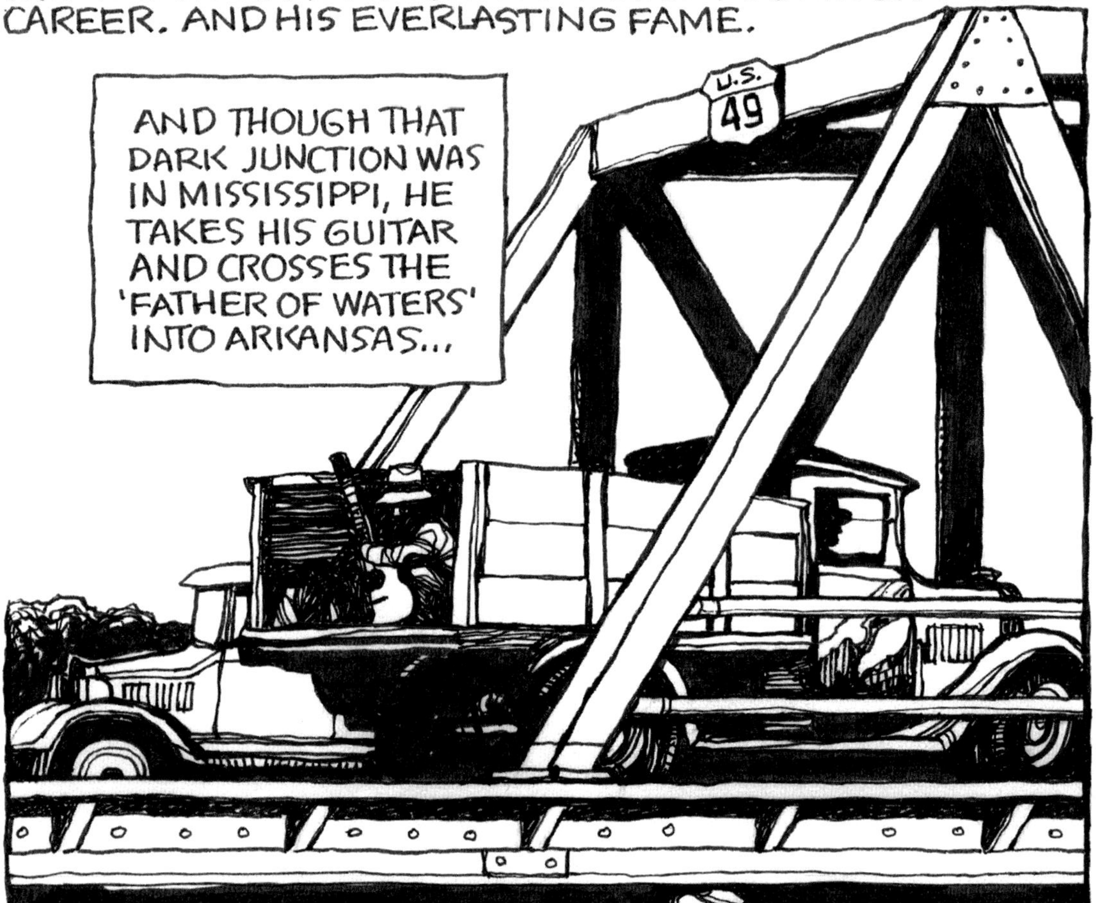

U.S. 49
AND THOUGH THAT DARK JUNCTION WAS IN MISSISSIPPI, HE TAKES HIS GUITAR AND CROSSES THE 'FATHER OF WATERS' INTO ARKANSAS...

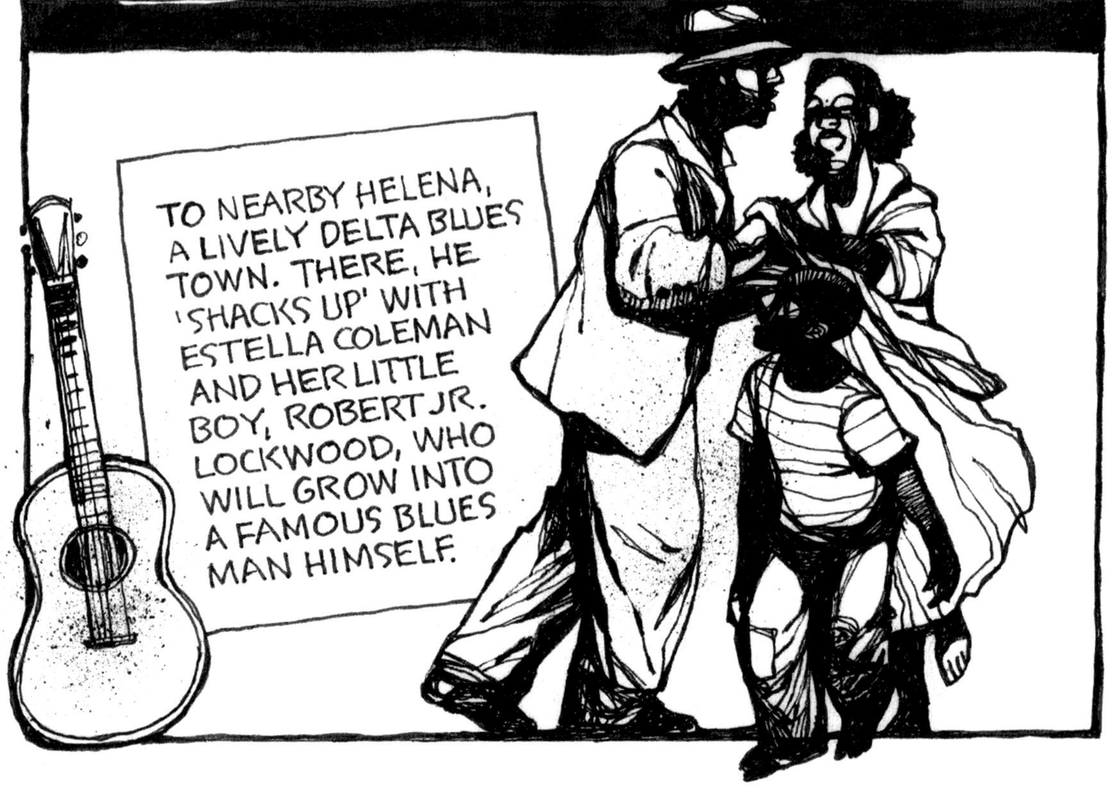

TO NEARBY HELENA, A LIVELY DELTA BLUES TOWN. THERE, HE 'SHACKS UP' WITH ESTELLA COLEMAN AND HER LITTLE BOY, ROBERT JR. LOCKWOOD, WHO WILL GROW INTO A FAMOUS BLUES MAN HIMSELF.

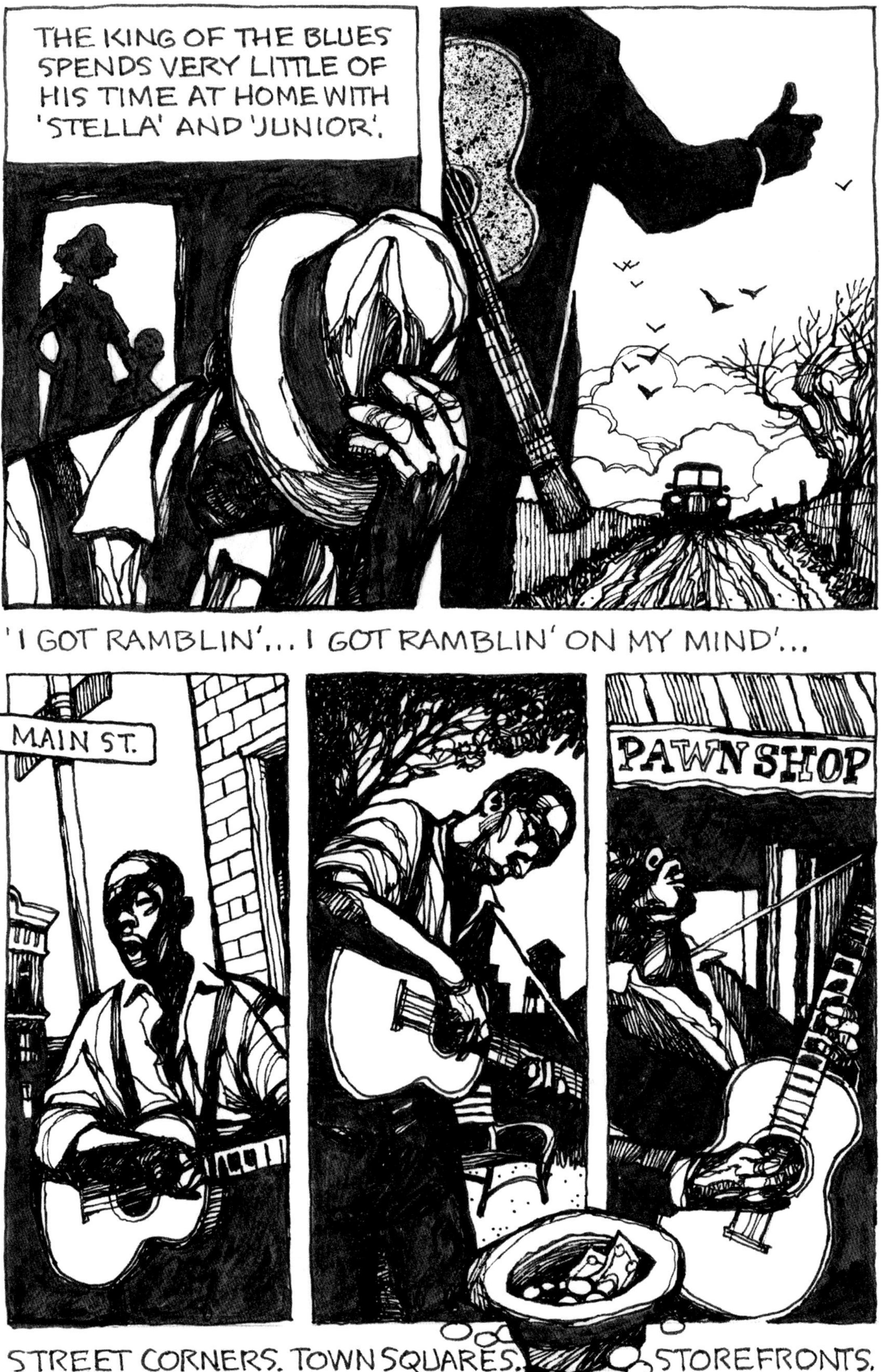
THE KING OF THE BLUES SPENDS VERY LITTLE OF HIS TIME AT HOME WITH 'STELLA' AND 'JUNIOR'.
'I GOT RAMBLIN'... I GOT RAMBLIN' ON MY MIND'...
MAIN ST.
PAWN SHOP
STREET CORNERS. TOWN SQUARES. STOREFRONTS.

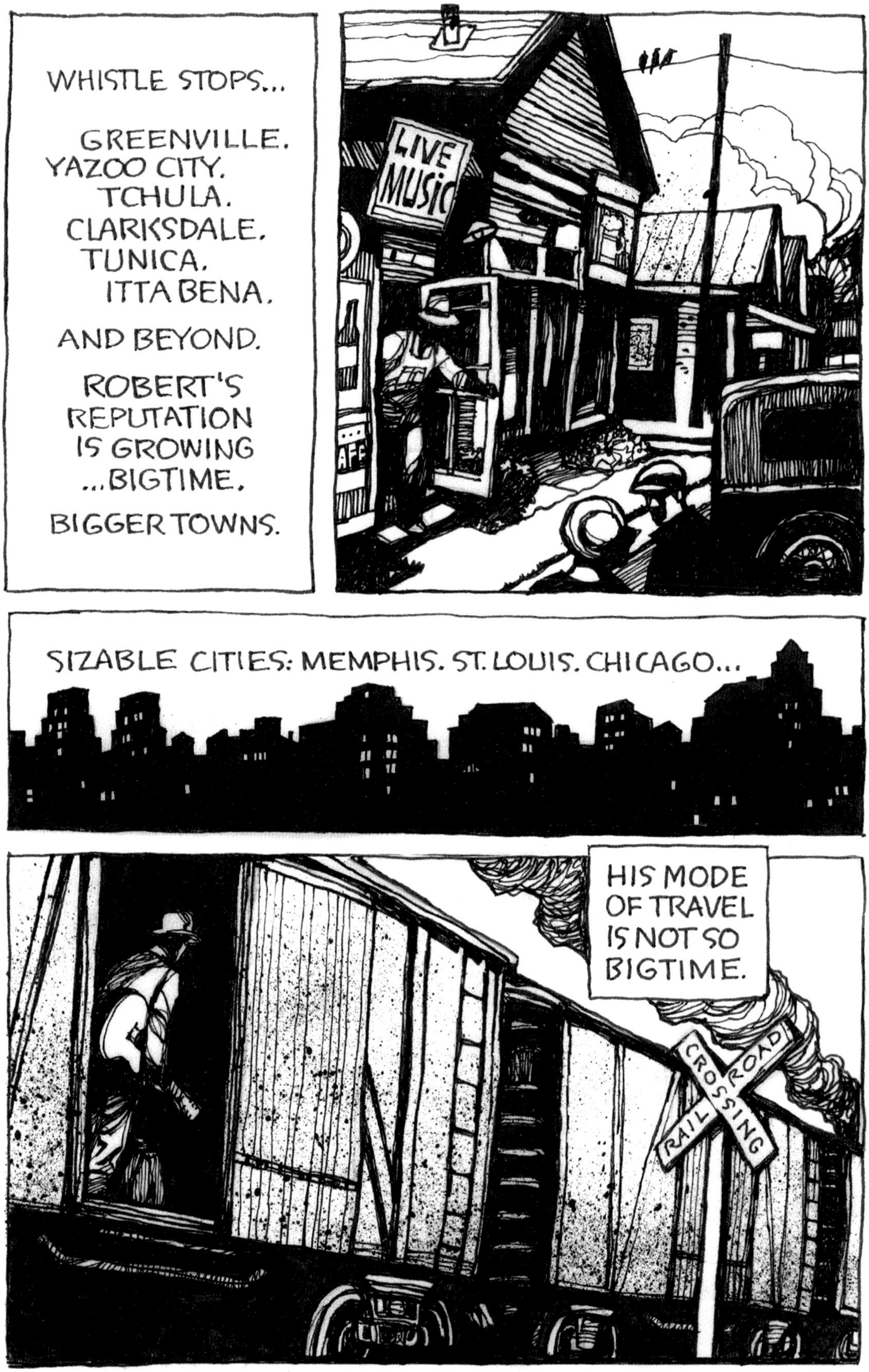
WHISTLE STOPS...
GREENVILLE.
YAZOO CITY.
TCHULA.
CLARKSDALE.
TUNICA.
ITTA BENA.
AND BEYOND.
ROBERT'S REPUTATION IS GROWING ...BIGTIME.
BIGGER TOWNS.
LIVE MUSIC
SIZABLE CITIES: MEMPHIS. ST. LOUIS. CHICAGO...
HIS MODE OF TRAVEL IS NOT SO BIGTIME.
RAIL ROAD CROSSING

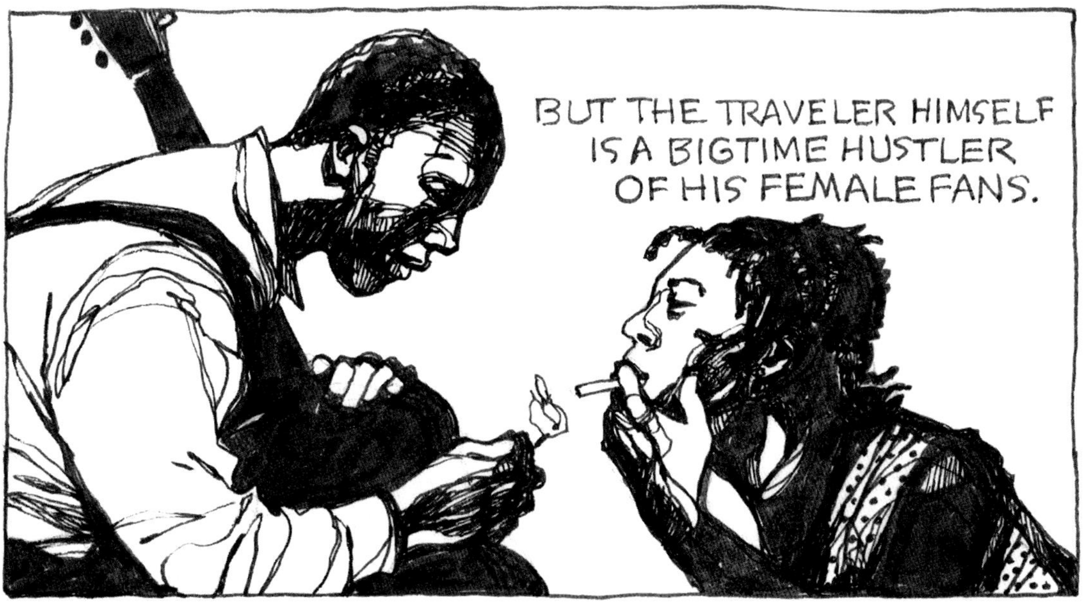
BUT THE TRAVELER HIMSELF
IS A BIGTIME HUSTLER
OF HIS FEMALE FANS.

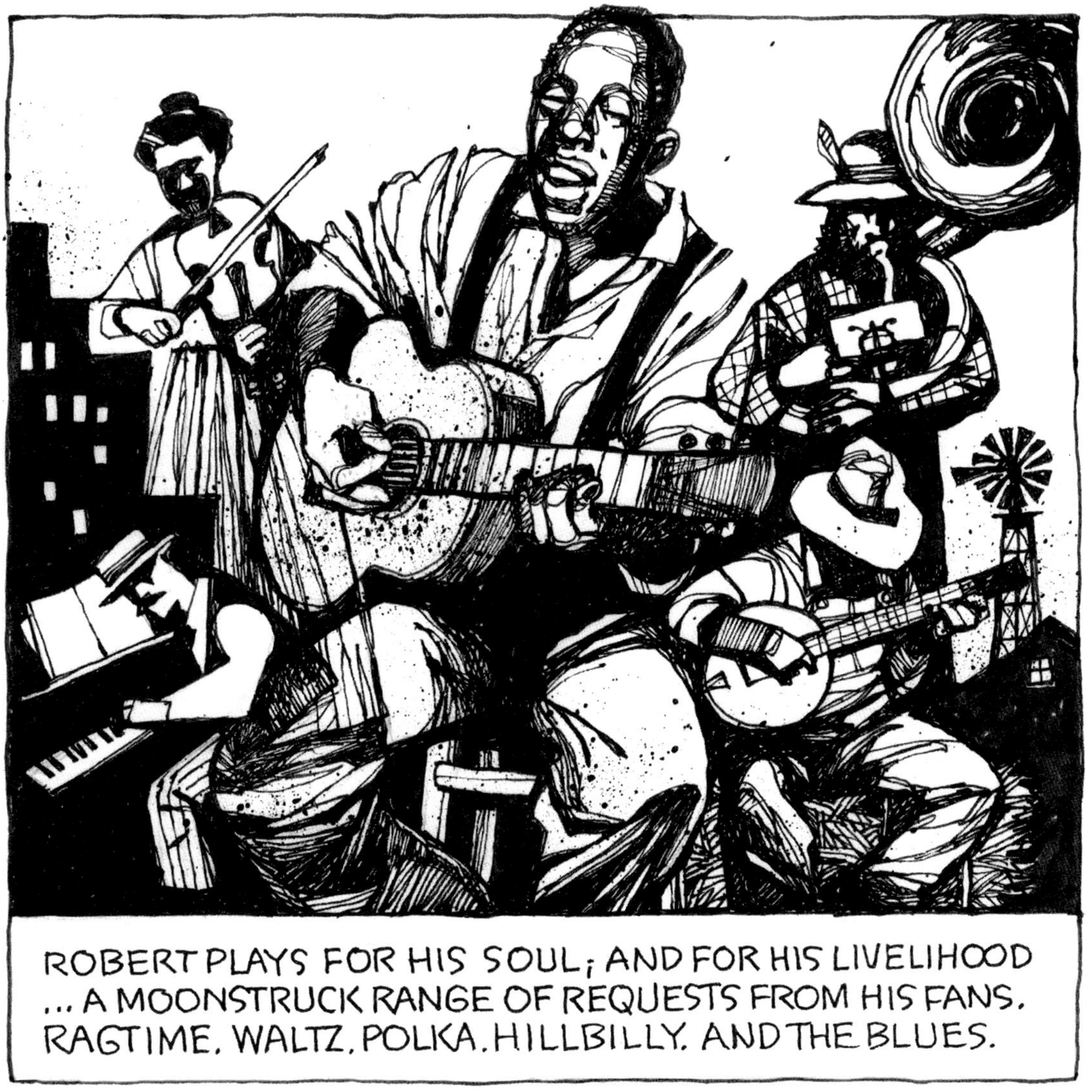
ROBERT PLAYS FOR HIS SOUL; AND FOR HIS LIVELIHOOD
... A MOONSTRUCK RANGE OF REQUESTS FROM HIS FANS.
RAGTIME. WALTZ. POLKA. HILLBILLY. AND THE BLUES.

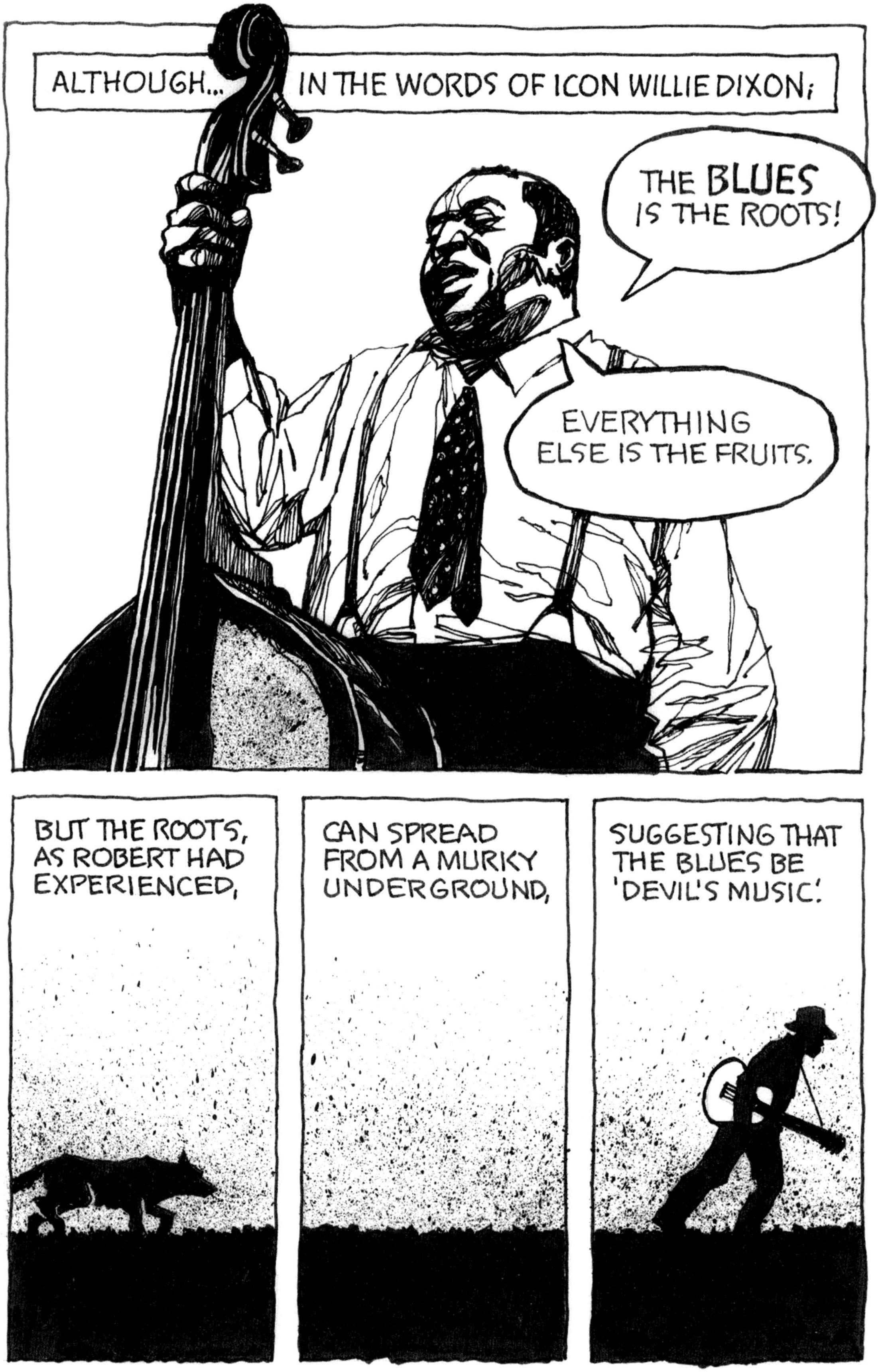
ALTHOUGH... IN THE WORDS OF ICON WILLIE DIXON;
THE BLUES IS THE ROOTS!
EVERYTHING ELSE IS THE FRUITS.
BUT THE ROOTS, AS ROBERT HAD EXPERIENCED,
CAN SPREAD FROM A MURKY UNDERGROUND,
SUGGESTING THAT THE BLUES BE 'DEVIL'S MUSIC.'

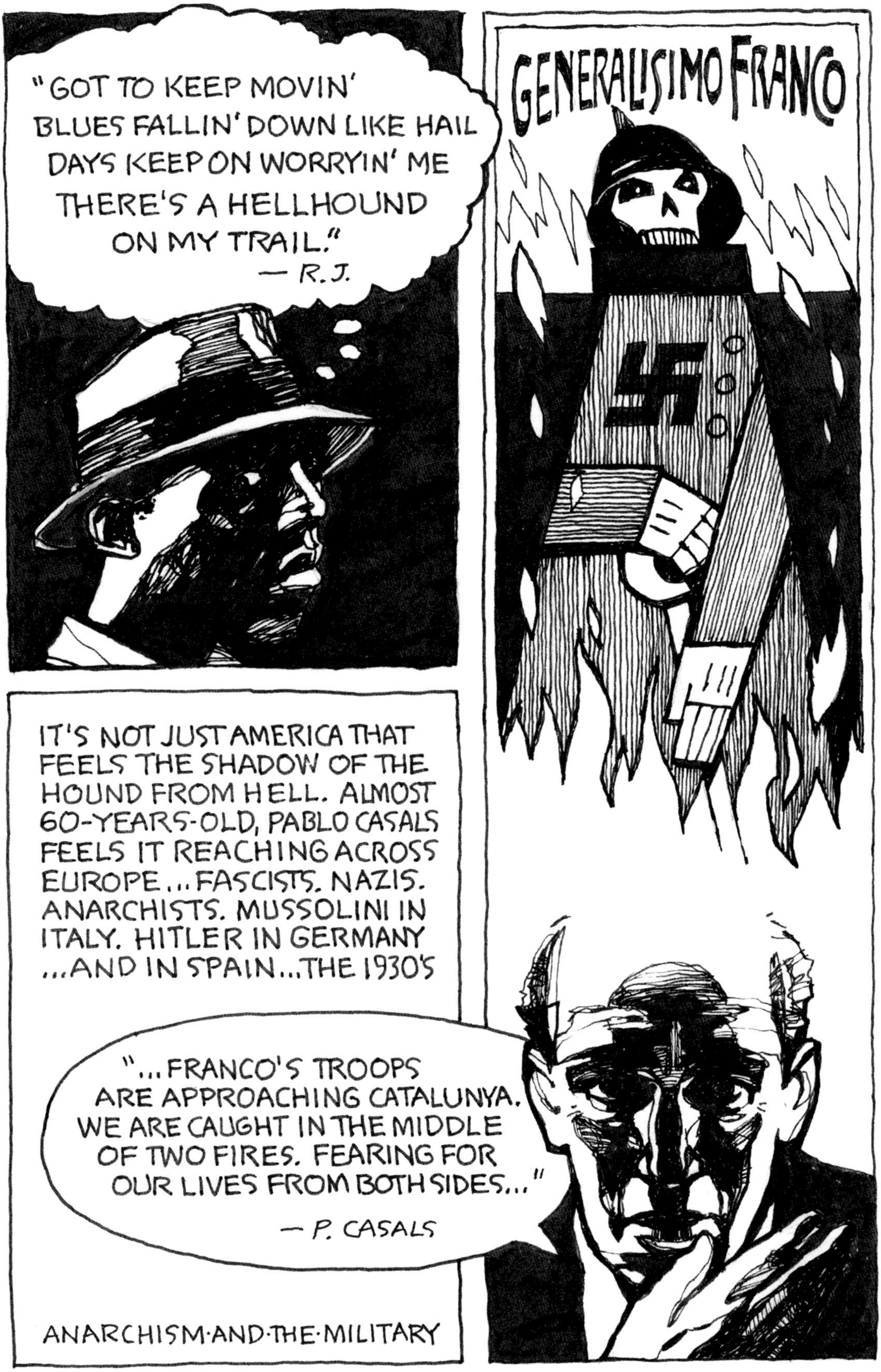
"GOT TO KEEP MOVIN' BLUES FALLIN' DOWN LIKE HAIL DAYS KEEP ON WORRYIN' ME THERE'S A HELLHOUND ON MY TRAIL." — R.J.
GENERALISIMO FRANCO
IT'S NOT JUST AMERICA THAT FEELS THE SHADOW OF THE HOUND FROM HELL. ALMOST 60-YEARS-OLD, PABLO CASALS FEELS IT REACHING ACROSS EUROPE... FASCISTS. NAZIS. ANARCHISTS. MUSSOLINI IN ITALY. HITLER IN GERMANY ...AND IN SPAIN...THE 1930'S
"...FRANCO'S TROOPS ARE APPROACHING CATALUNYA. WE ARE CAUGHT IN THE MIDDLE OF TWO FIRES. FEARING FOR OUR LIVES FROM BOTH SIDES..." — P. CASALS
ANARCHISM·AND·THE·MILITARY

PABLO'S HOMELAND HAS BEEN THE SPANISH REPUBLIC SINCE 1931, WHEN KING ALFONSO DEPARTED. LIKE HIS LATE PAPA CARLOS, THE CELLIST SUPPORTS SOCIALIST REPUBLICANS, HOPING FOR A CATALAN AUTONOMY.

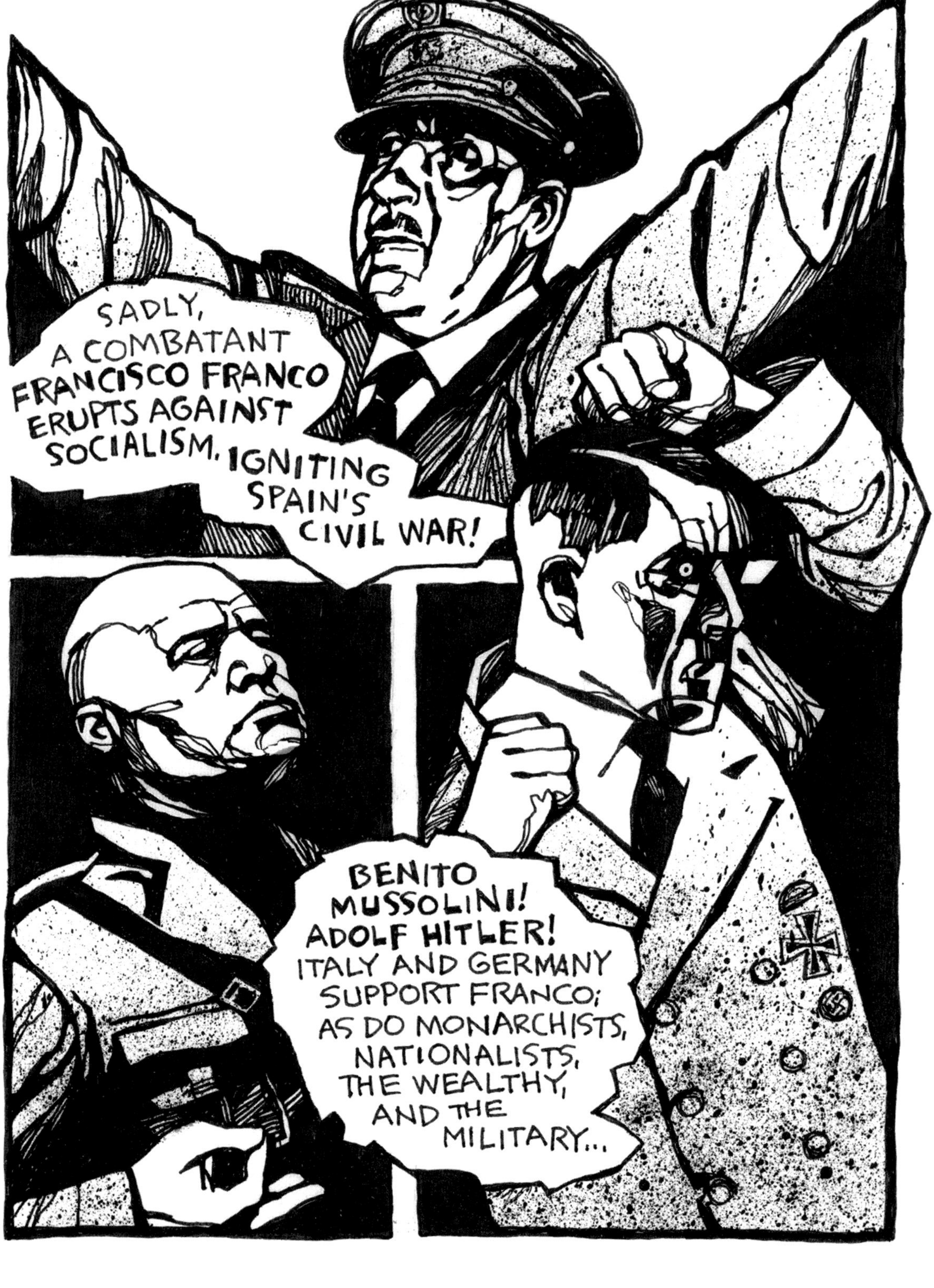

SADLY, A COMBATANT **FRANCISCO FRANCO** ERUPTS AGAINST SOCIALISM, IGNITING SPAIN'S CIVIL WAR!
BENITO MUSSOLINI! ADOLF HITLER! ITALY AND GERMANY SUPPORT FRANCO; AS DO MONARCHISTS, NATIONALISTS, THE WEALTHY, AND THE MILITARY...

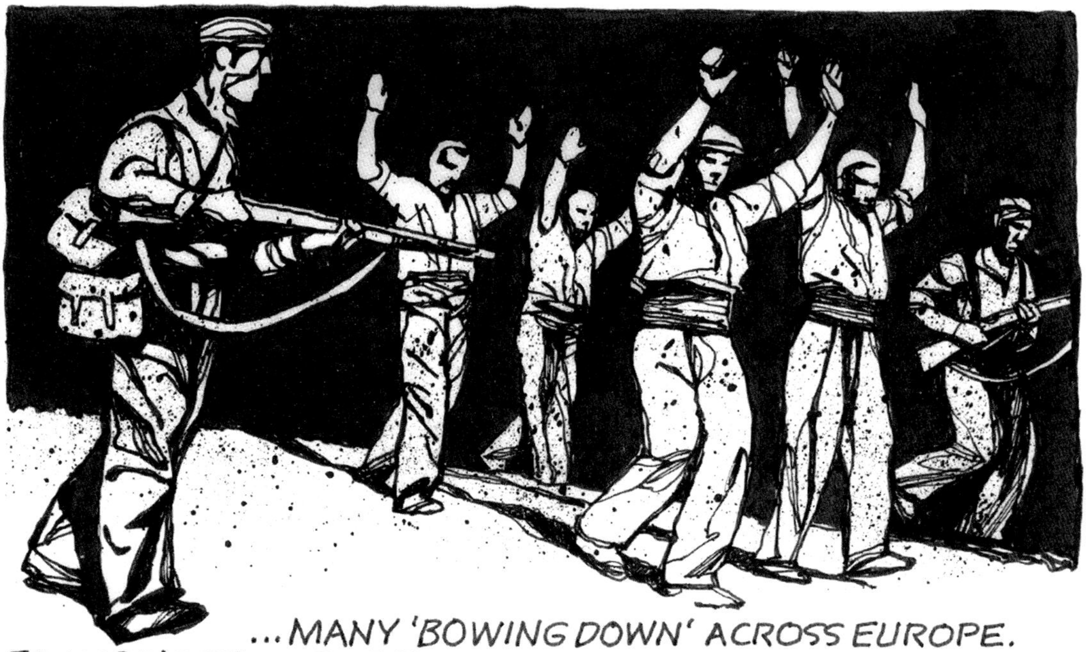

...MANY 'BOWING DOWN' ACROSS EUROPE.
FRANCO'S TROOPS REPRESSING SOCIALIST REPUBLICANS.

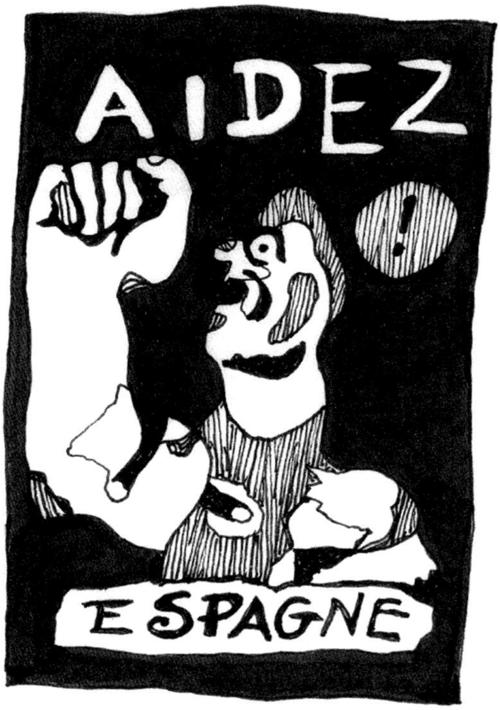
AIDEZ
ESPAGNE

BUT NOT ALL 'BOW DOWN.'
FAMED SPANISH ARTIST
JOAN MIRO, LIKE CASALS,
A CREATIVE CATALAN,
RESPONDS WITH HIS
CLASSIC POSTER
'SUPPORT SPAIN'

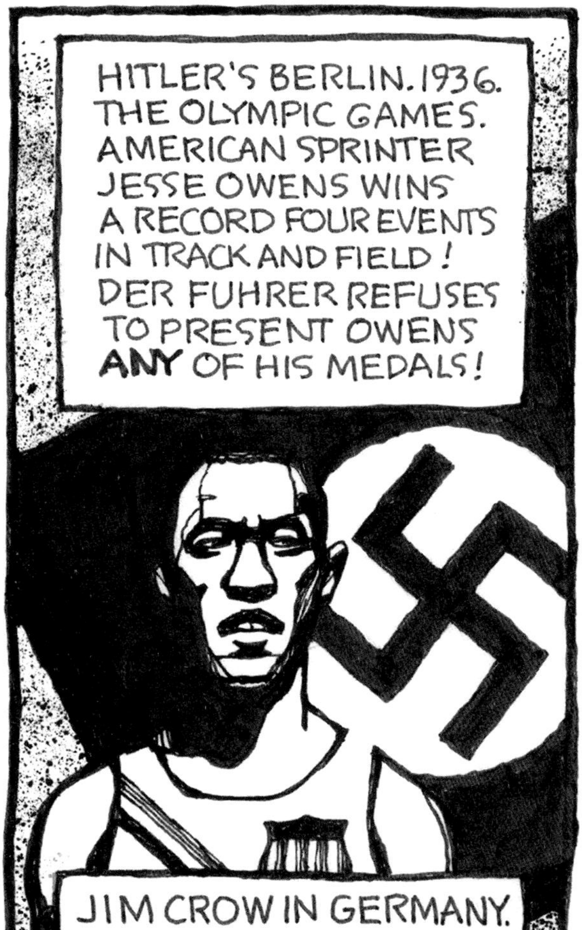
HITLER'S BERLIN. 1936.
THE OLYMPIC GAMES.
AMERICAN SPRINTER
JESSE OWENS WINS
A RECORD FOUR EVENTS
IN TRACK AND FIELD!
DER FUHRER REFUSES
TO PRESENT OWENS
ANY OF HIS MEDALS!
JIM CROW IN GERMANY.

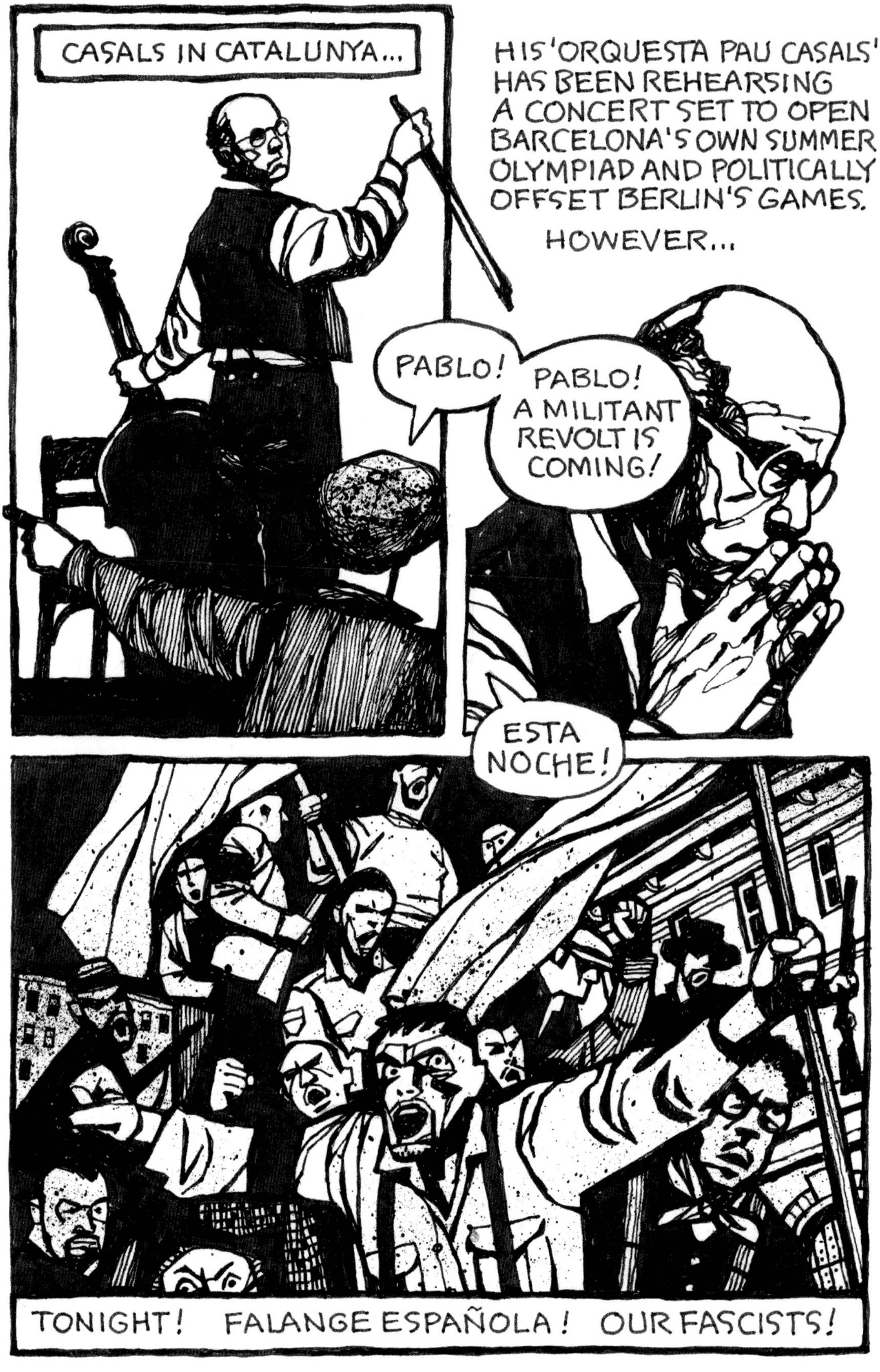
CASALS IN CATALUNYA...
HIS 'ORQUESTA PAU CASALS' HAS BEEN REHEARSING A CONCERT SET TO OPEN BARCELONA'S OWN SUMMER OLYMPIAD AND POLITICALLY OFFSET BERLIN'S GAMES.
HOWEVER...
PABLO!
PABLO! A MILITANT REVOLT IS COMING!
ESTA NOCHE!
TONIGHT! FALANGE ESPAÑOLA! OUR FASCISTS!

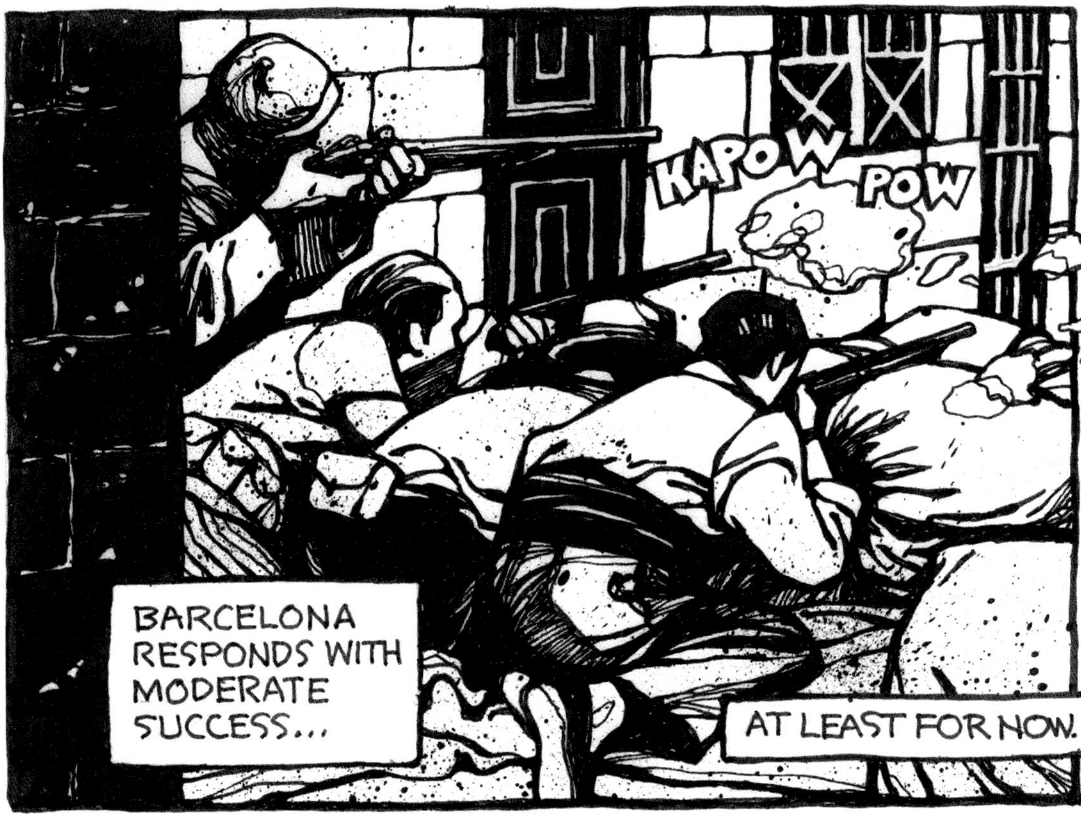
KAPOW
POW
BARCELONA RESPONDS WITH MODERATE SUCCESS...
AT LEAST FOR NOW.

BUT STILL, ACROSS SPAIN, INSURGENTS ARE A THREAT... INSPIRED SOMEWHAT BY THE NAZI DICTATOR AND BY THE PHILOSOPHY OF HIS MANIFESTO...

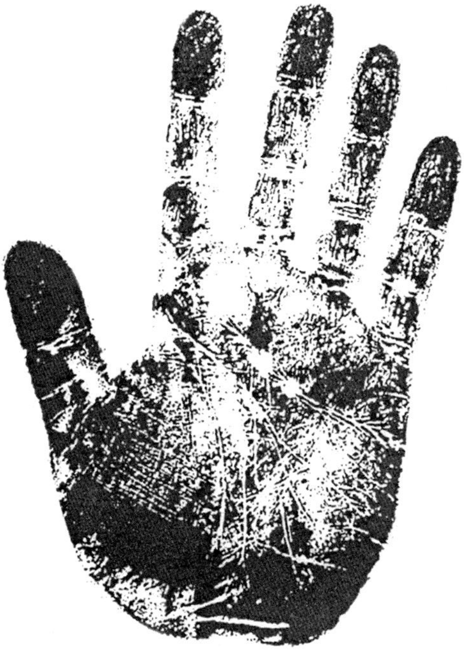

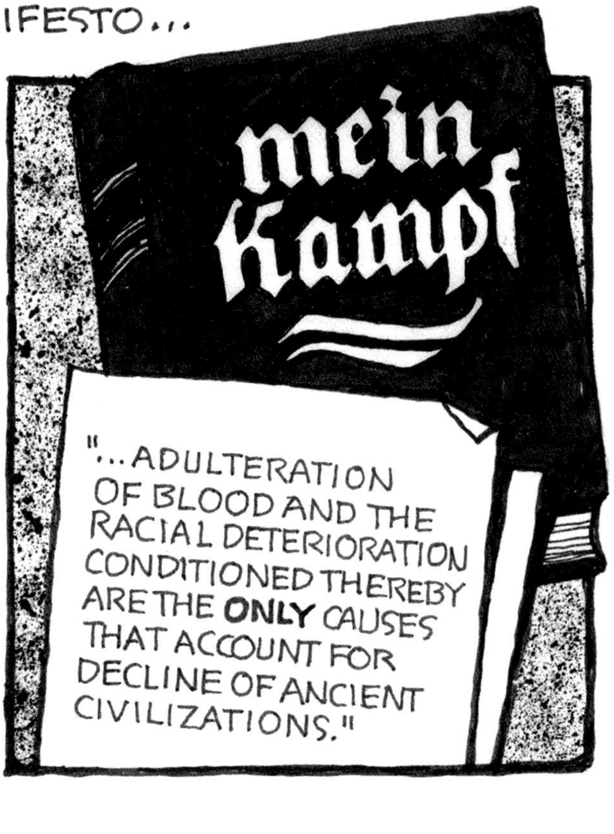
mein Kampf
"...ADULTERATION OF BLOOD AND THE RACIAL DETERIORATION CONDITIONED THEREBY ARE THE **ONLY** CAUSES THAT ACCOUNT FOR DECLINE OF ANCIENT CIVILIZATIONS."

IF PEOPLE ARE YOUNG, PURE WHITE GERMANS THEY HAVE MORE OF AN OPPORTUNITY TO GROW UP TO BE A NAZI ... AND TO BE NASTY. HOWEVER, IF ONE IS YOUNG AND JEWISH. A PERSON OF COLOR. OR AN OLDER SPANISH REPUBLICAN, THEY WILL GROW UP IGNORANT, INDECENT, SAYS MEIN KAMPF.

... ANNE FRANK. JESSE OWENS. ROBERT JOHNSON. PABLO CASALS.

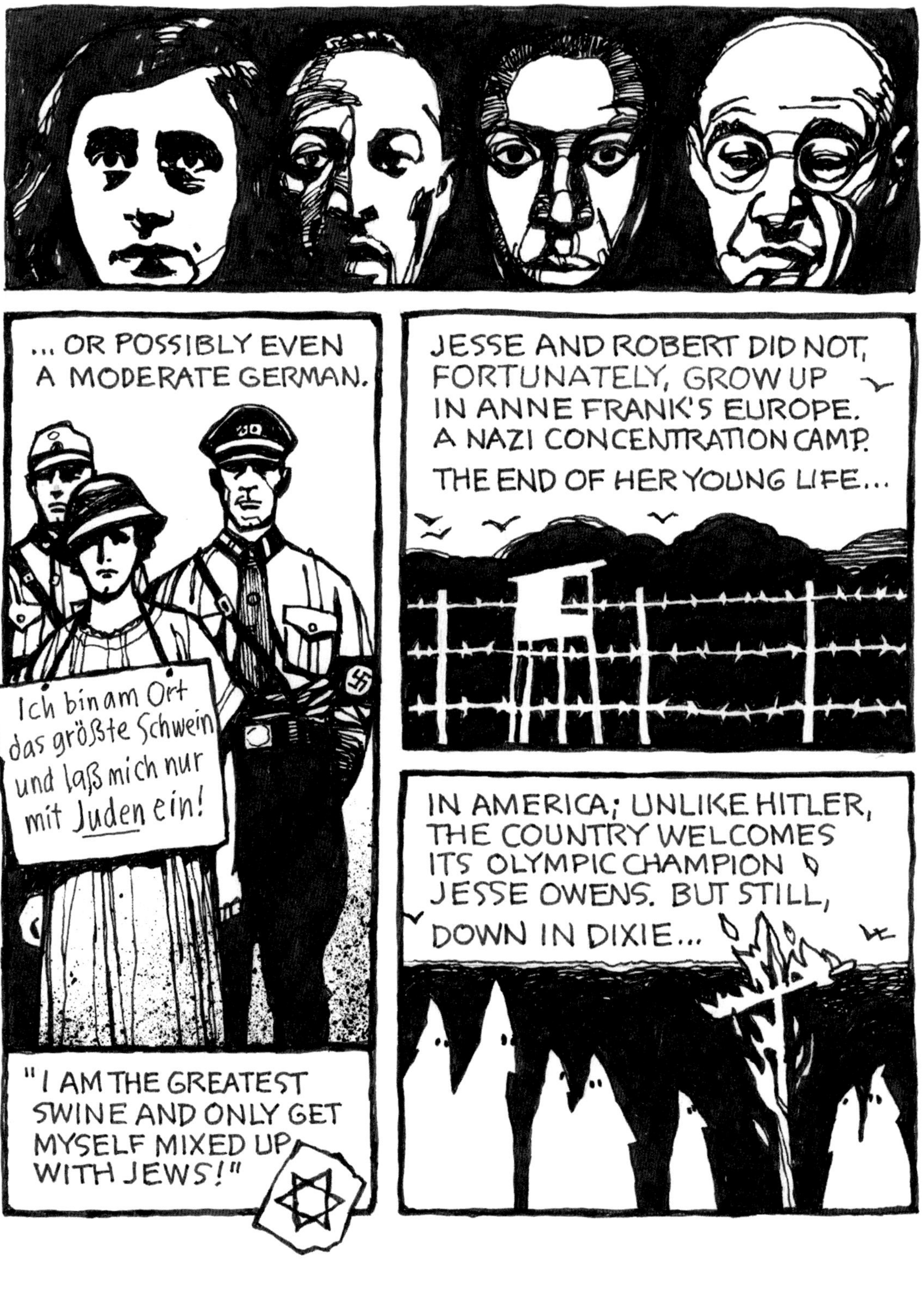

... OR POSSIBLY EVEN A MODERATE GERMAN.
Ich bin am Ort das größte Schwein und laß mich nur mit Juden ein!
"I AM THE GREATEST SWINE AND ONLY GET MYSELF MIXED UP WITH JEWS!"
JESSE AND ROBERT DID NOT, FORTUNATELY, GROW UP IN ANNE FRANK'S EUROPE. A NAZI CONCENTRATION CAMP.
THE END OF HER YOUNG LIFE...
IN AMERICA; UNLIKE HITLER, THE COUNTRY WELCOMES ITS OLYMPIC CHAMPION JESSE OWENS. BUT STILL,
DOWN IN DIXIE...

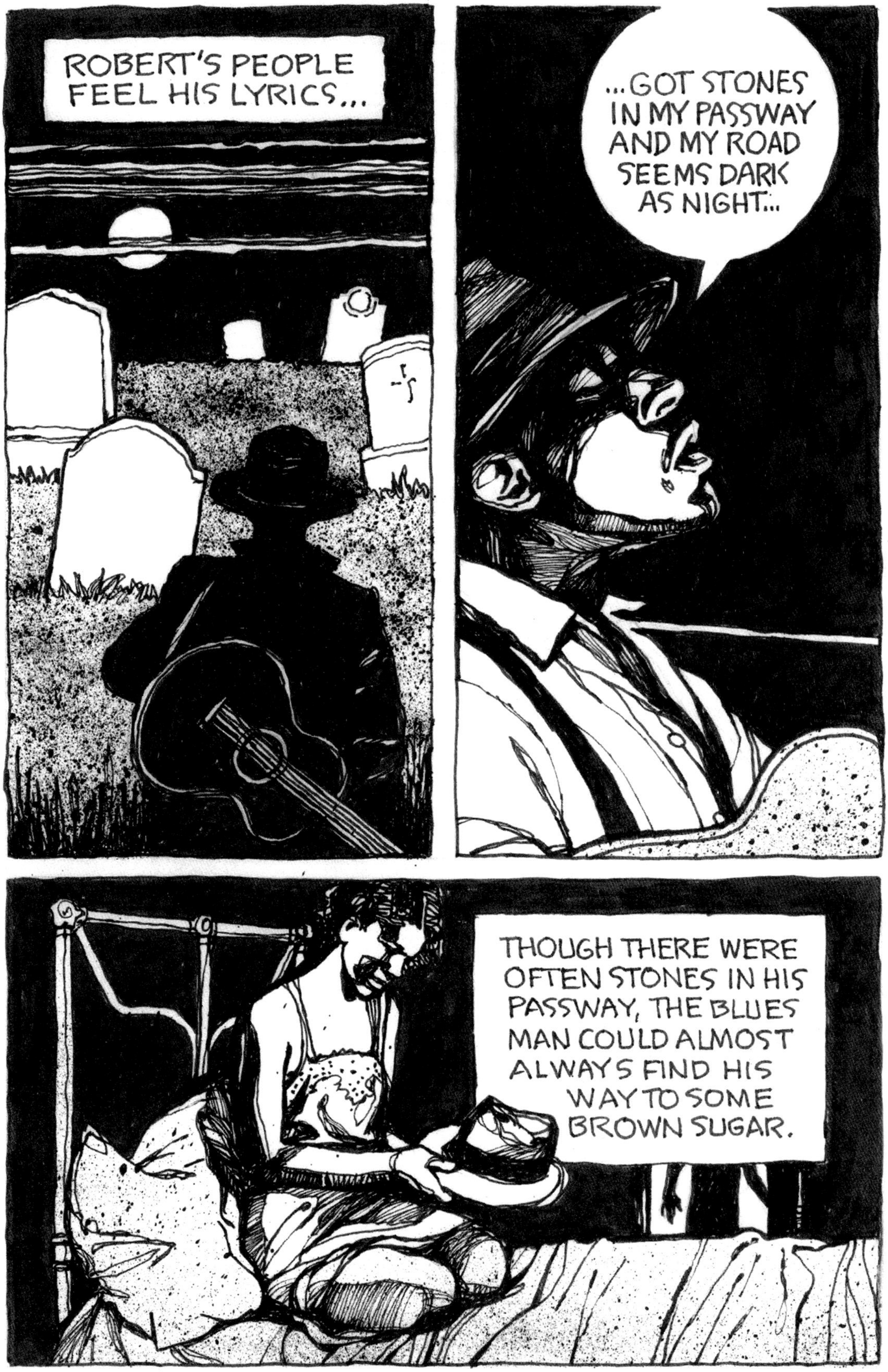
ROBERT'S PEOPLE FEEL HIS LYRICS...
...GOT STONES IN MY PASSWAY AND MY ROAD SEEMS DARK AS NIGHT...
THOUGH THERE WERE OFTEN STONES IN HIS PASSWAY, THE BLUES MAN COULD ALMOST ALWAYS FIND HIS WAY TO SOME BROWN SUGAR.

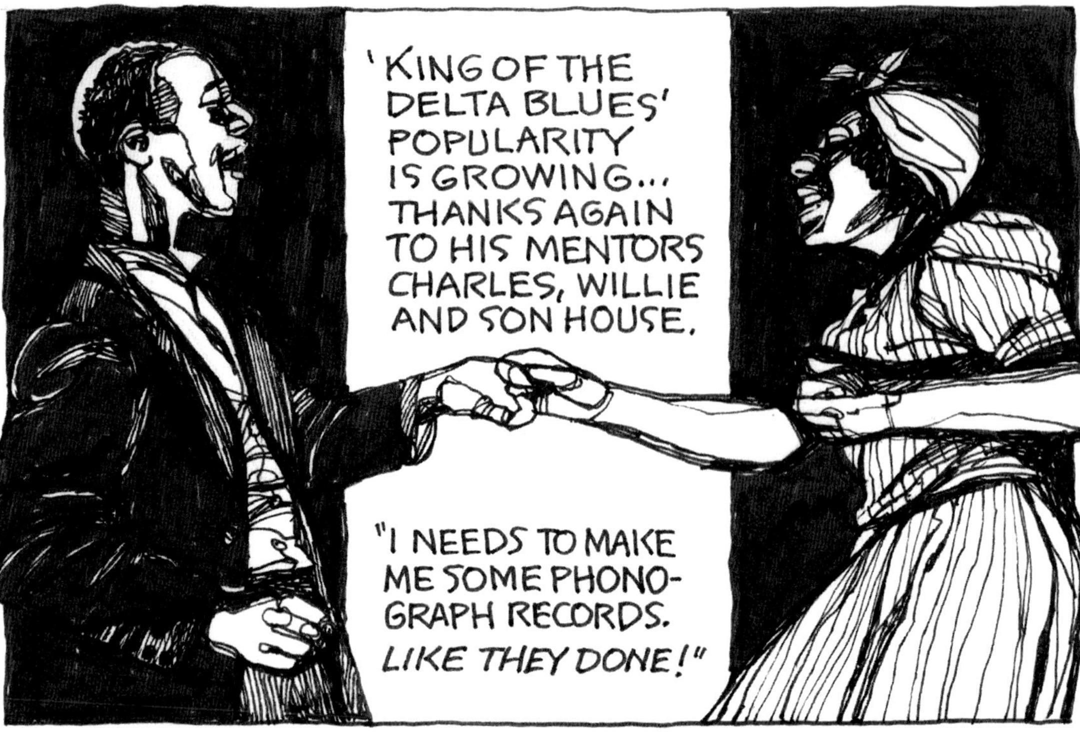
'KING OF THE DELTA BLUES' POPULARITY IS GROWING... THANKS AGAIN TO HIS MENTORS CHARLES, WILLIE AND SON HOUSE.
"I NEEDS TO MAKE ME SOME PHONOGRAPH RECORDS. *LIKE THEY DONE!*"

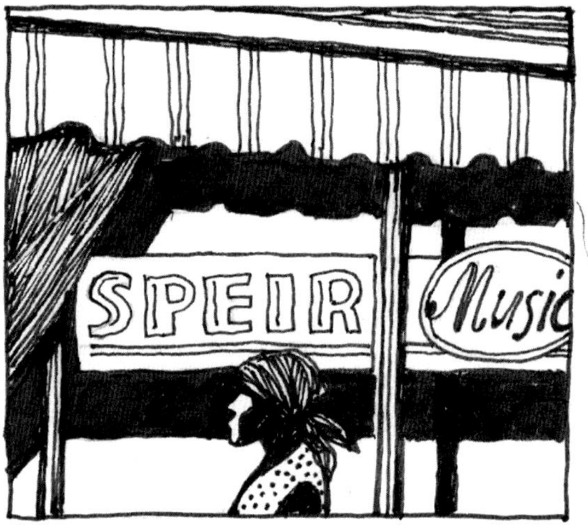
SPEIR
Music

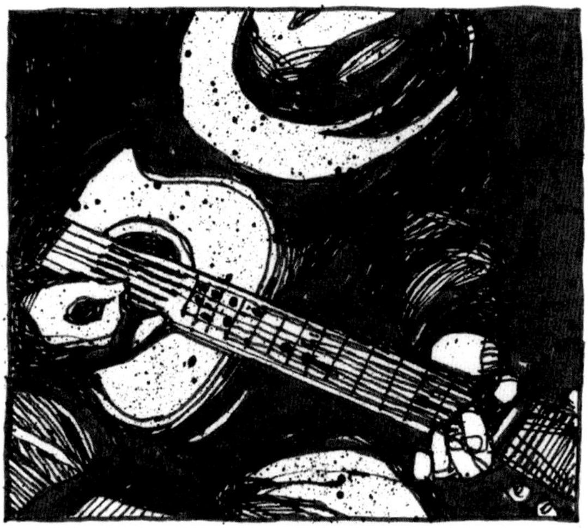

ROBERT CONNECTS WITH H.C. SPEIR AT HIS MUSIC STORE IN JACKSON, MISSISSIPPI. HE AUDITIONS FOR SPEIR AND TALENT SCOUT ERNIE OERTLE. BOTH ARE IMPRESSED!

SOON AFTER, ERNIE AND ROBERT ARE HEADING WEST... ON THE ROAD TO SAN ANTONIO, AND A RECORDING SESSION.

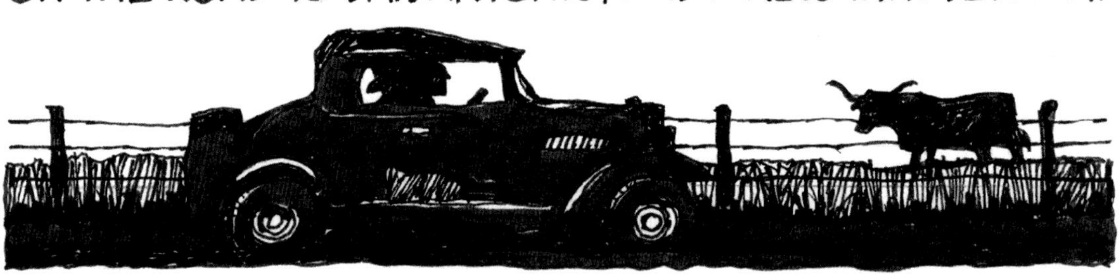

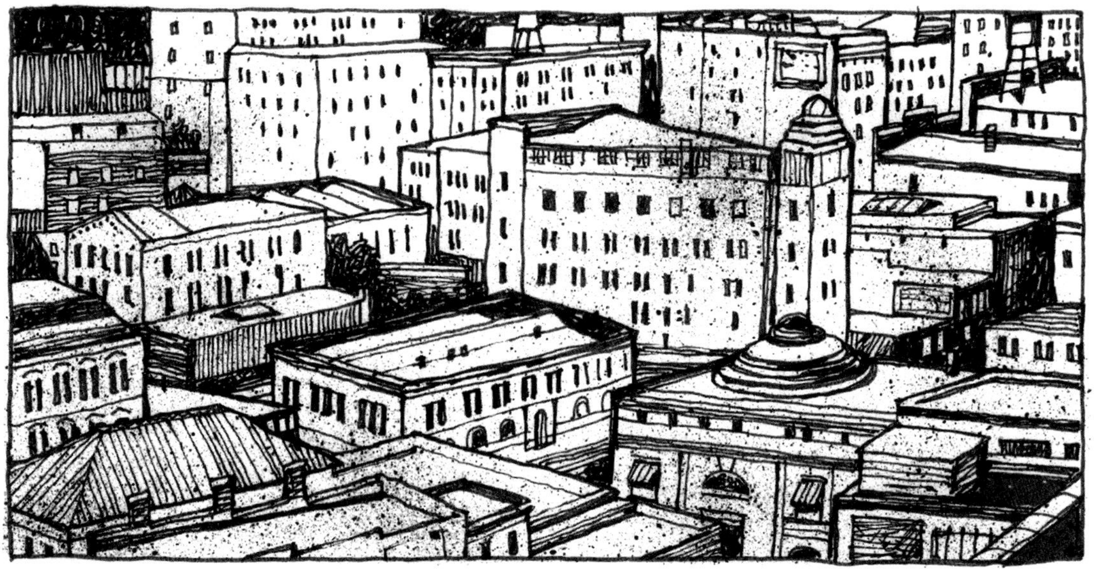

THE THIRD WEEK IN NOVEMBER. 1936...

THE GUNTER HOTEL IN DOWNTOWN SAN ANTONIO, TEXAS. HISTORICALLY. IRONICALLY. THE REGIONAL BASE FOR ANOTHER ROBERT FROM THE SOUTH DURING HIS CIVIL WAR.

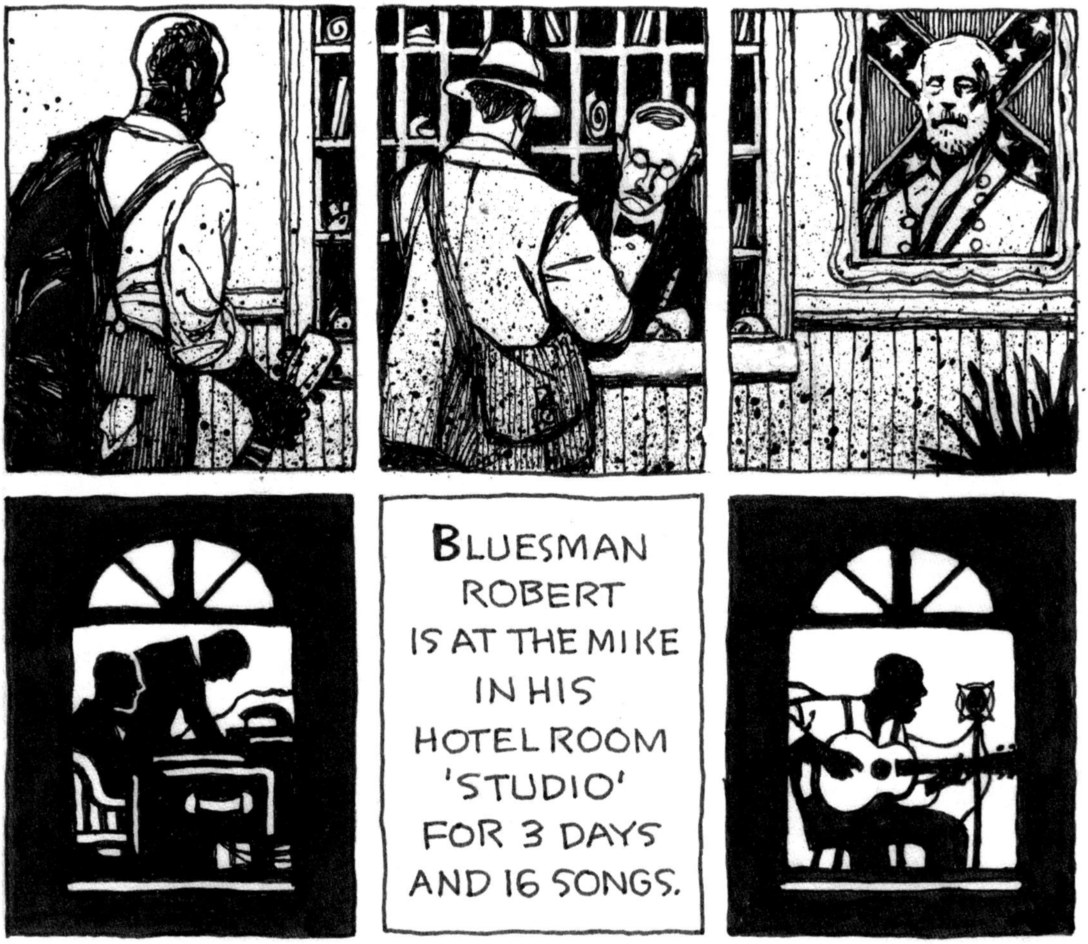
BLUESMAN ROBERT IS AT THE MIKE IN HIS HOTEL ROOM 'STUDIO' FOR 3 DAYS AND 16 SONGS.

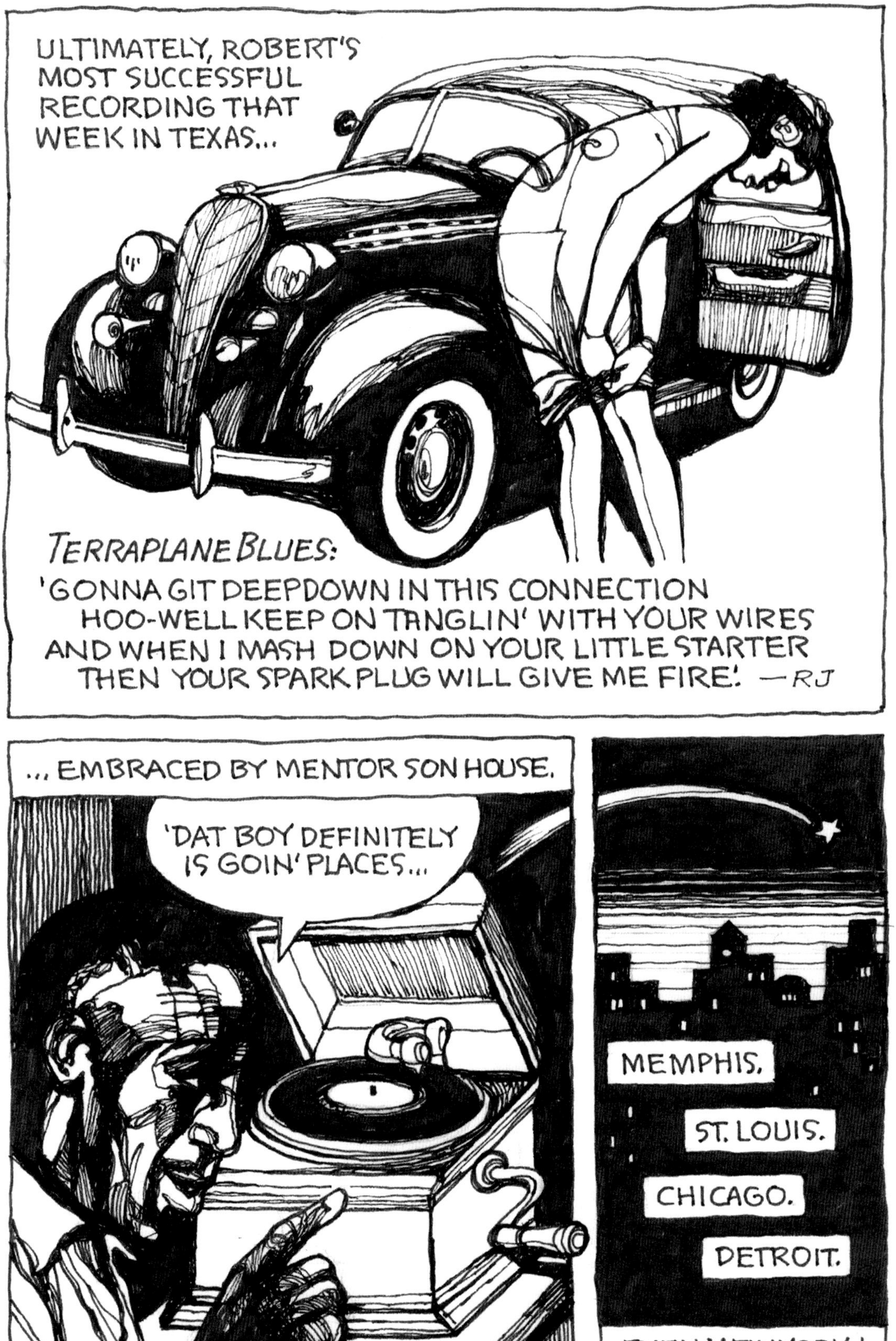
ULTIMATELY, ROBERT'S MOST SUCCESSFUL RECORDING THAT WEEK IN TEXAS...
TERRAPLANE BLUES:
'GONNA GIT DEEPDOWN IN THIS CONNECTION
HOO-WELL KEEP ON TANGLIN' WITH YOUR WIRES
AND WHEN I MASH DOWN ON YOUR LITTLE STARTER
THEN YOUR SPARK PLUG WILL GIVE ME FIRE.' —RJ
... EMBRACED BY MENTOR SON HOUSE.
'DAT BOY DEFINITELY IS GOIN' PLACES...
MEMPHIS.
ST. LOUIS.
CHICAGO.
DETROIT.
EVEN NEW YORK!

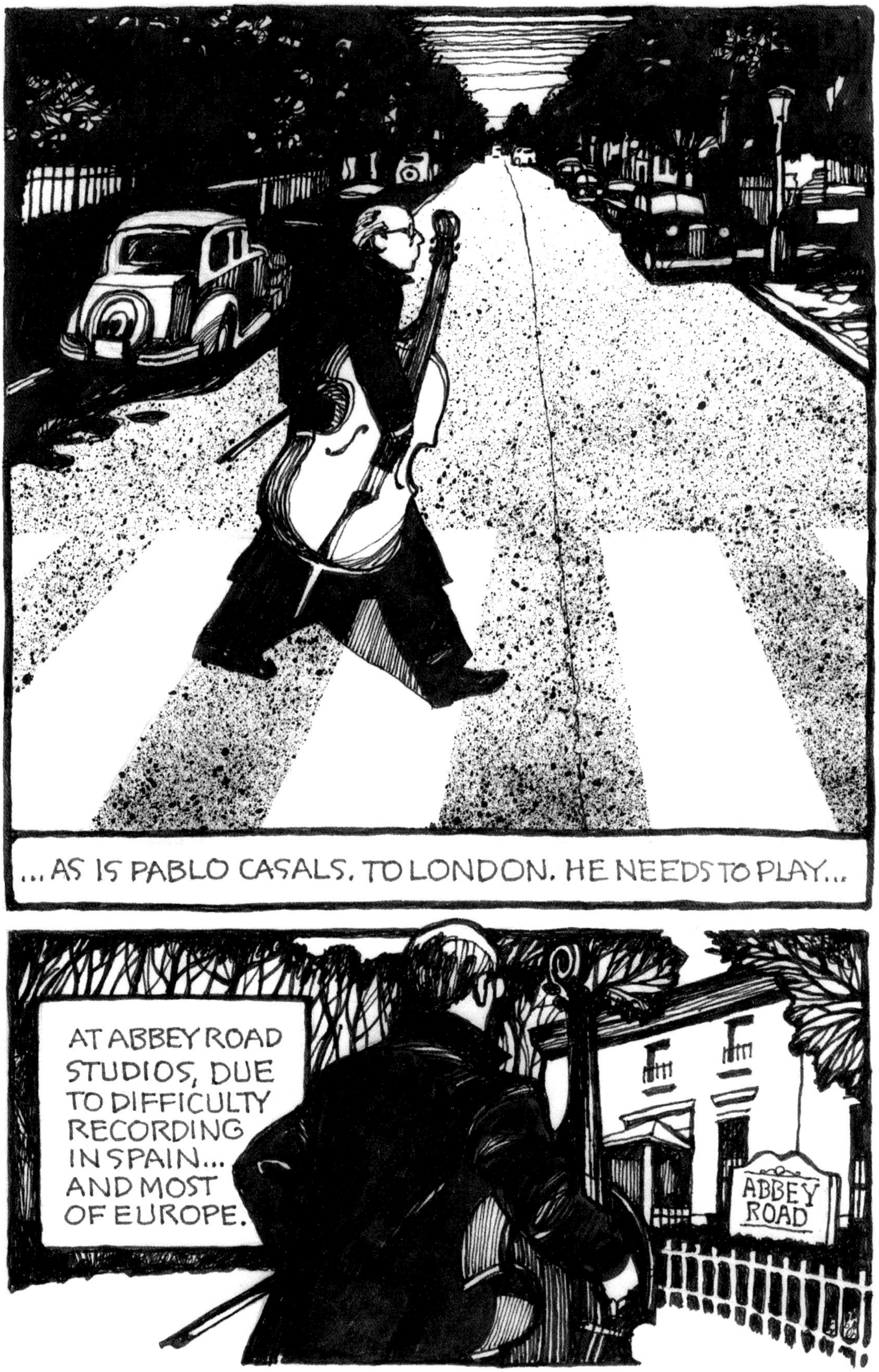
...AS IS PABLO CASALS. TO LONDON. HE NEEDS TO PLAY...
AT ABBEY ROAD STUDIOS, DUE TO DIFFICULTY RECORDING IN SPAIN... AND MOST OF EUROPE.
ABBEY ROAD

LONDON. THE THIRD WEEK OF NOVEMBER. 1936.

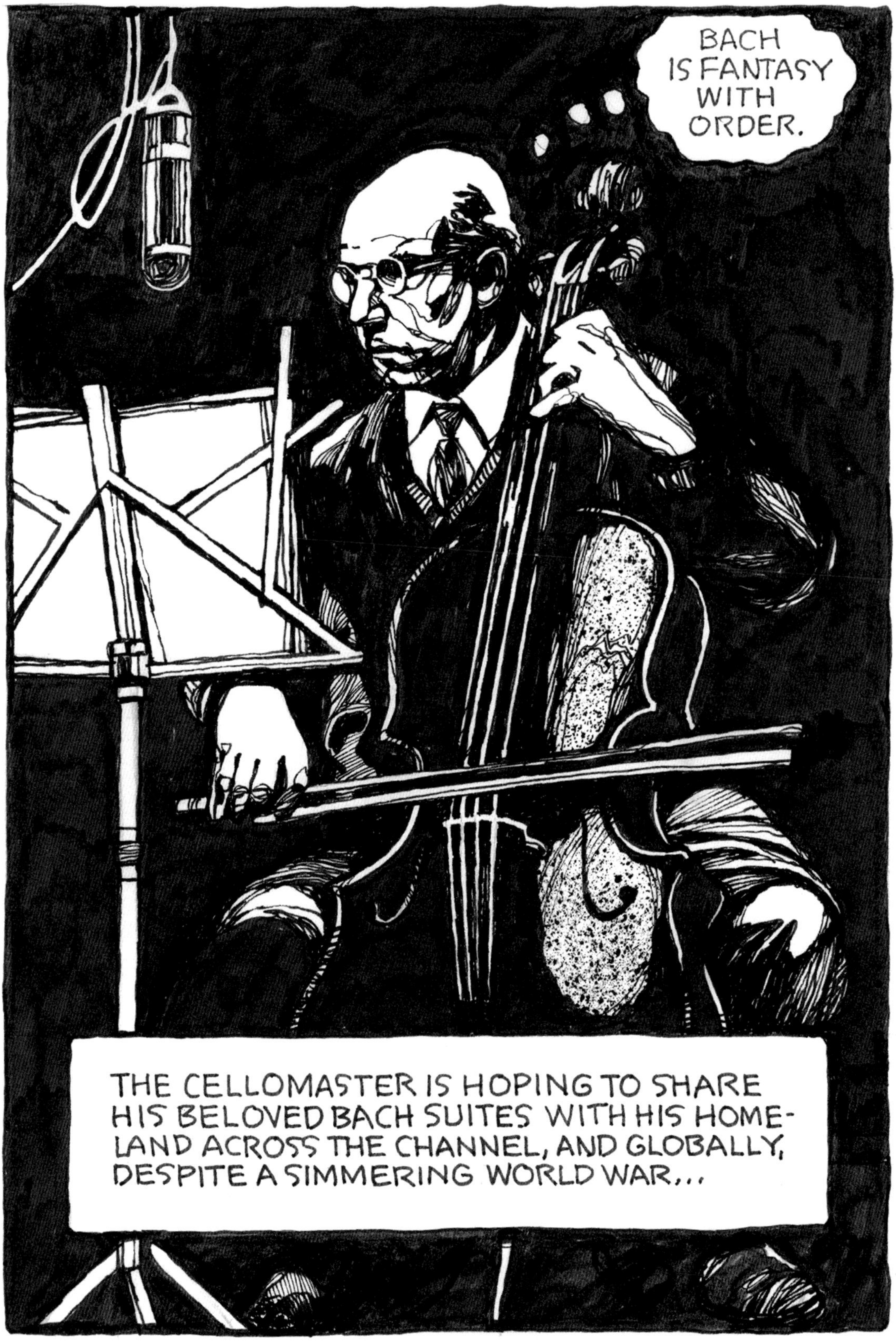
BACH IS FANTASY WITH ORDER.
THE CELLOMASTER IS HOPING TO SHARE HIS BELOVED BACH SUITES WITH HIS HOME-LAND ACROSS THE CHANNEL, AND GLOBALLY, DESPITE A SIMMERING WORLD WAR...

SAN ANTONIO. **SAME WEEK** IN NOVEMBER!

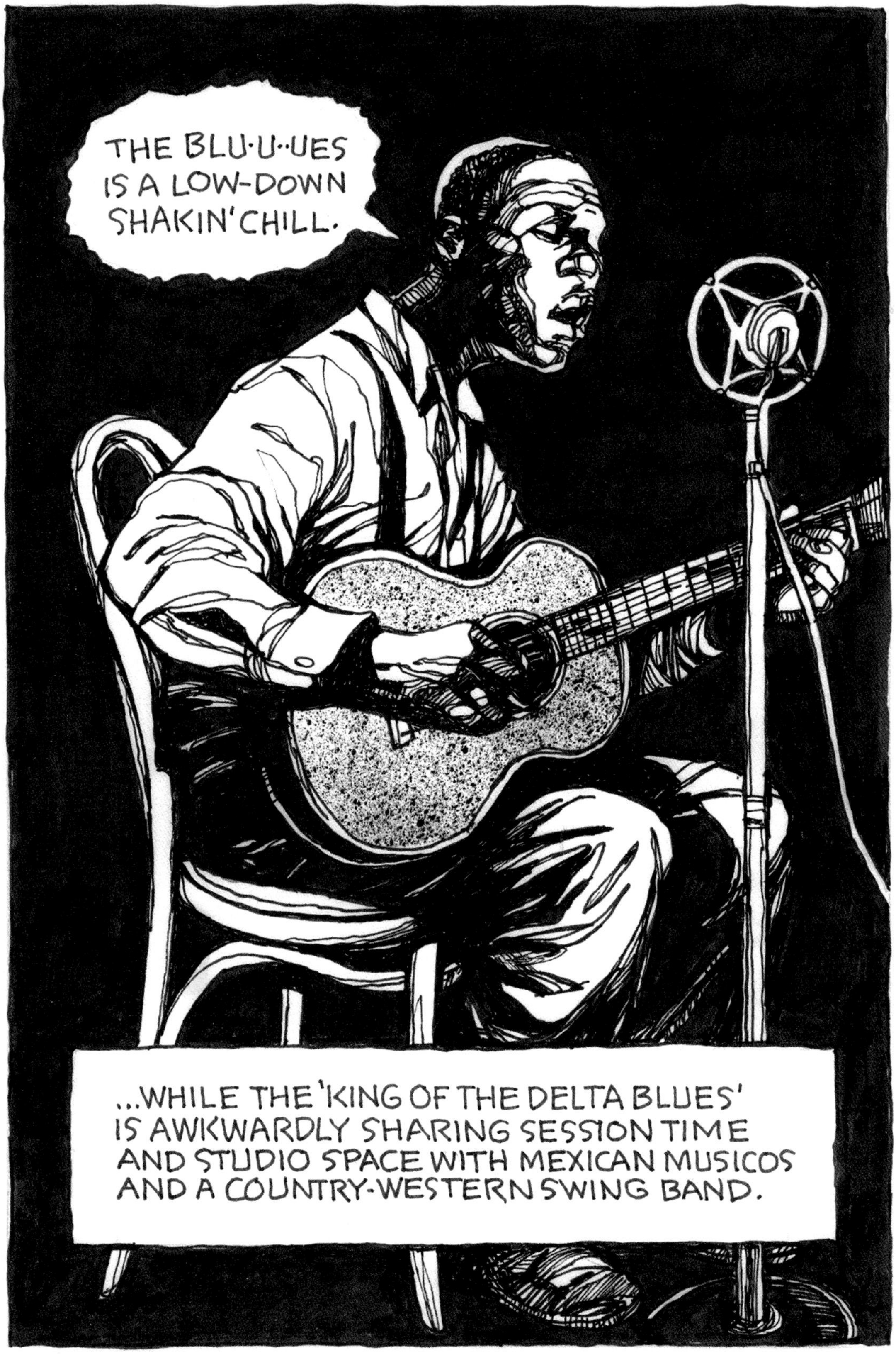
THE BLU·U··UES IS A LOW-DOWN SHAKIN' CHILL.
...WHILE THE 'KING OF THE DELTA BLUES' IS AWKWARDLY SHARING SESSION TIME AND STUDIO SPACE WITH MEXICAN MUSICOS AND A COUNTRY-WESTERN SWING BAND.

BOTH NOVEMBER SESSIONS HAVE A GREAT IMPACT ON OUR MUSIC, DESPITE SOME 'PERSONAL ISSUES.'

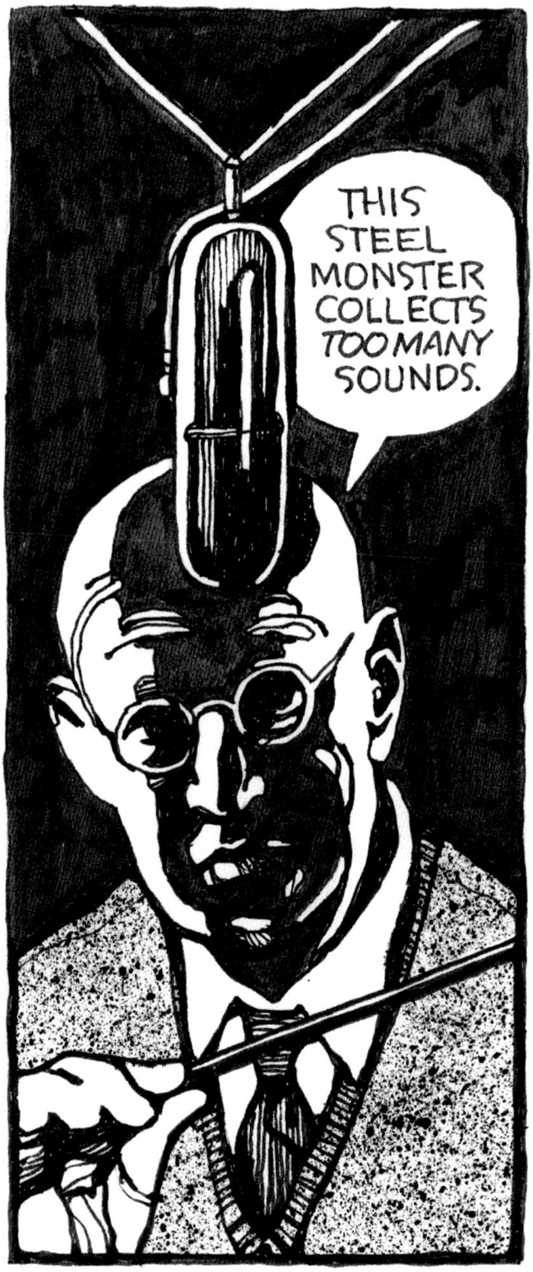
THIS STEEL MONSTER COLLECTS *TOO MANY* SOUNDS.

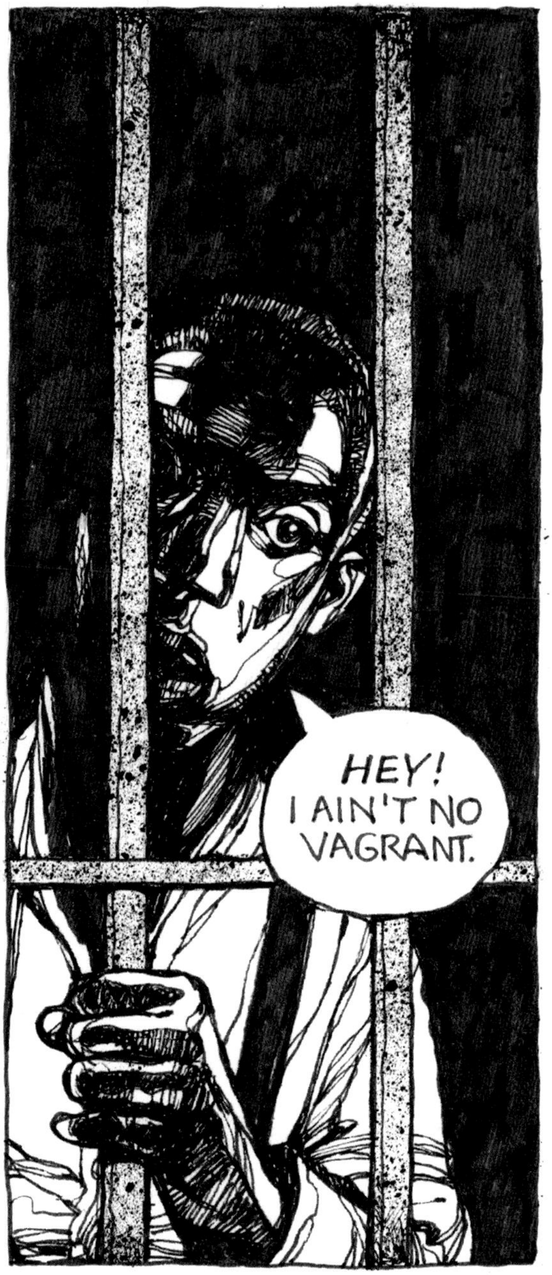
HEY! I AIN'T NO VAGRANT.

PABLO, IN FRONT OF A MICROPHONE, SELDOM HAS CONFIDENCE IN THAT TECHNOLOGY.

ROBERT, BEHIND BARS. OVERNIGHT. VAGRANCY. ASLEEP ON THE STREET IN SAN ANTONIO.

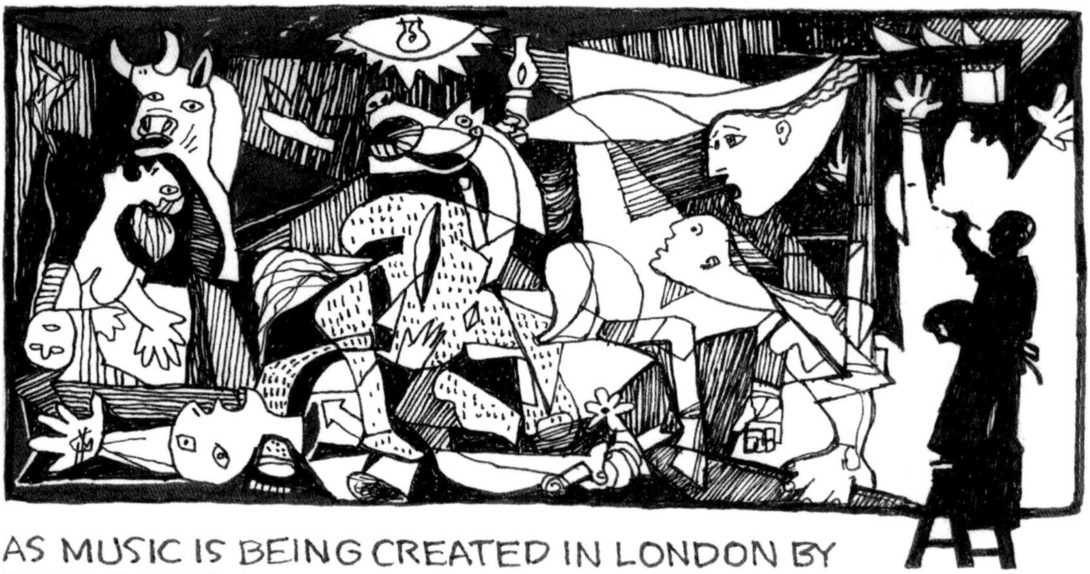

AS MUSIC IS BEING CREATED IN LONDON BY PABLO THE CELLIST, MADRID IS BESIEGED BY FRANCO'S MILITARY. FORTUNATELY THE CITY SURVIVES. HOWEVER, THE SMALLER SPANISH CITY GUERNICA IS NOT SO LUCKY, BOMBED-OUT BY HITLER'S LUFTWAFFE. 1600 VICTIMS.

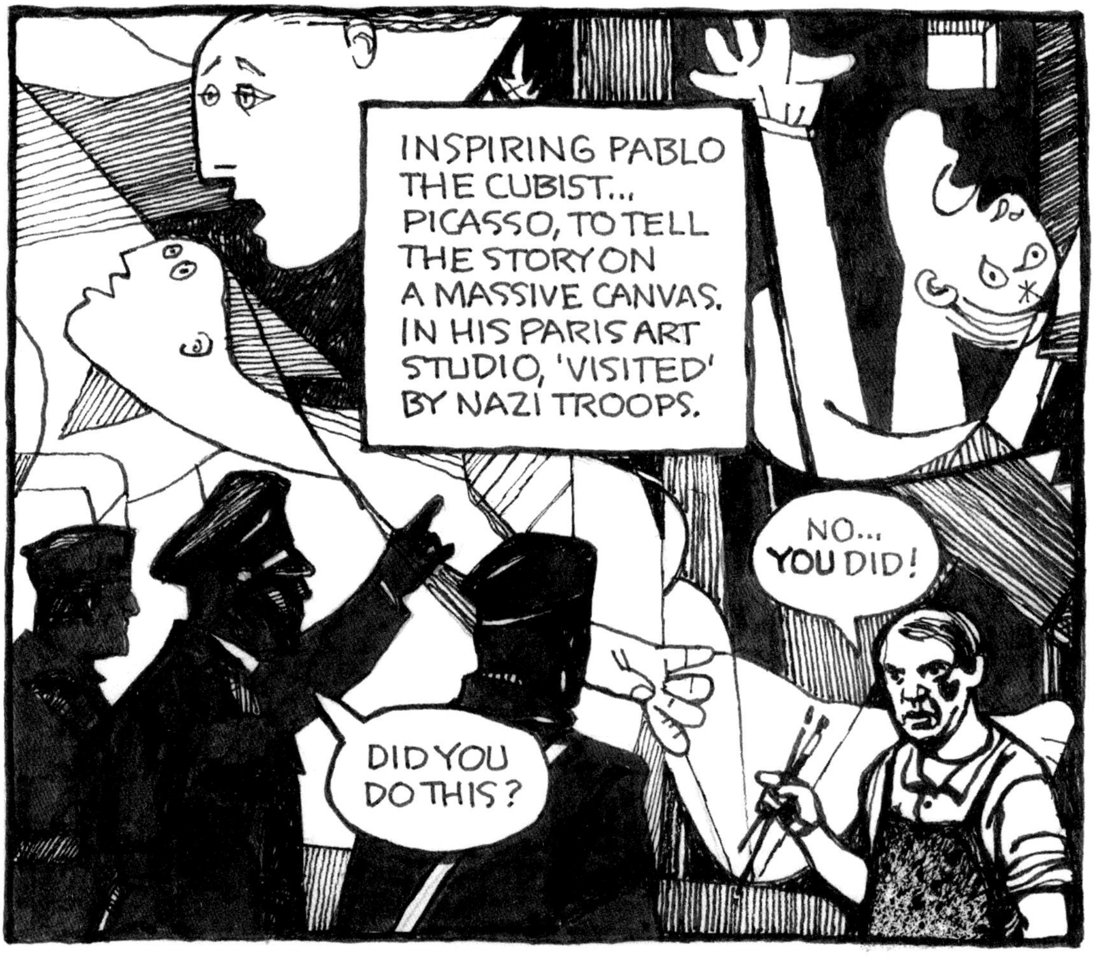
INSPIRING PABLO THE CUBIST... PICASSO, TO TELL THE STORY ON A MASSIVE CANVAS. IN HIS PARIS ART STUDIO, 'VISITED' BY NAZI TROOPS.
DID YOU DO THIS?
NO... **YOU** DID!

THAT YEAR 1937 HAS SEEN PICASSO PUT A HUMAN FACE ON THE HORROR OF WAR; AND THE BLUESMAN RETURN TO TEXAS. DALLAS. TO RECORD ANOTHER 15 SONGS.

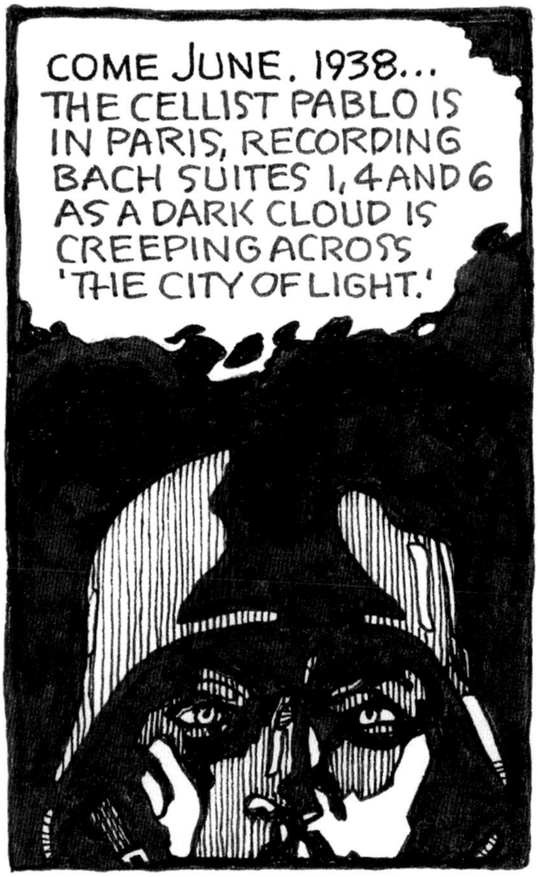
COME JUNE. 1938... THE CELLIST PABLO IS IN PARIS, RECORDING BACH SUITES 1, 4 AND 6 AS A DARK CLOUD IS CREEPING ACROSS 'THE CITY OF LIGHT.'

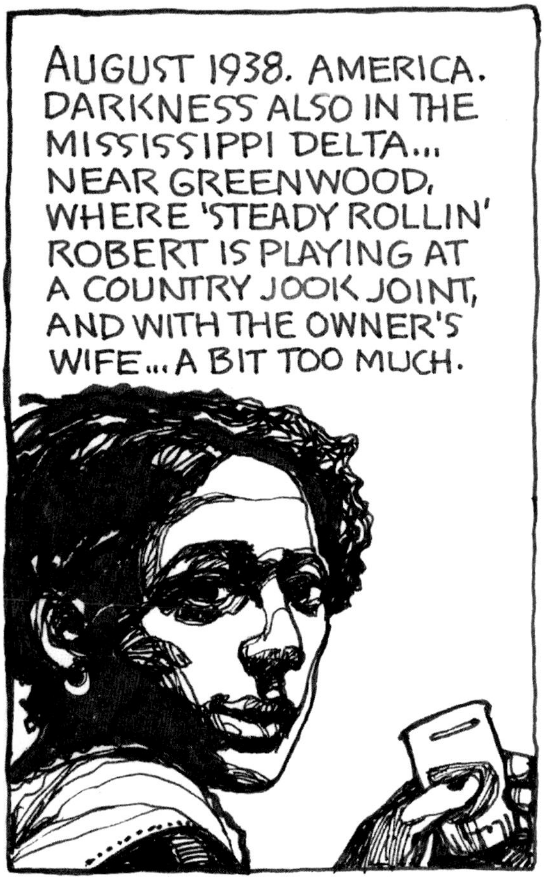
AUGUST 1938. AMERICA. DARKNESS ALSO IN THE MISSISSIPPI DELTA... NEAR GREENWOOD, WHERE 'STEADY ROLLIN' ROBERT IS PLAYING AT A COUNTRY JOOK JOINT, AND WITH THE OWNER'S WIFE... A BIT TOO MUCH.

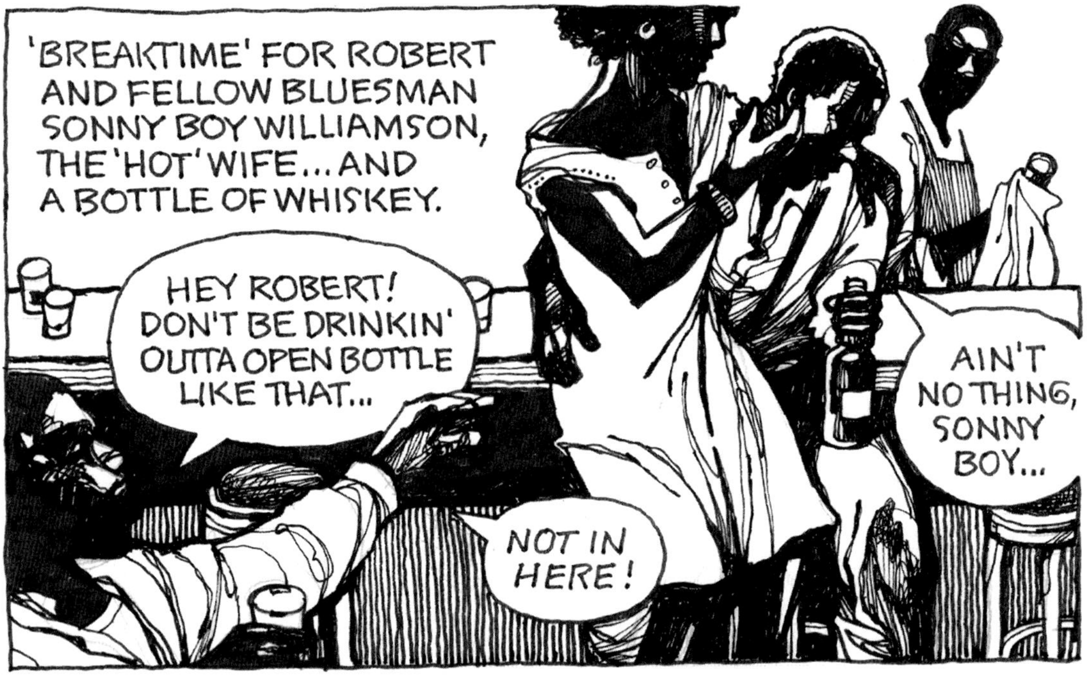
'BREAKTIME' FOR ROBERT AND FELLOW BLUESMAN SONNY BOY WILLIAMSON, THE 'HOT' WIFE... AND A BOTTLE OF WHISKEY.
HEY ROBERT! DON'T BE DRINKIN' OUTTA OPEN BOTTLE LIKE THAT...
NOT IN HERE!
AIN'T NO THING, SONNY BOY...

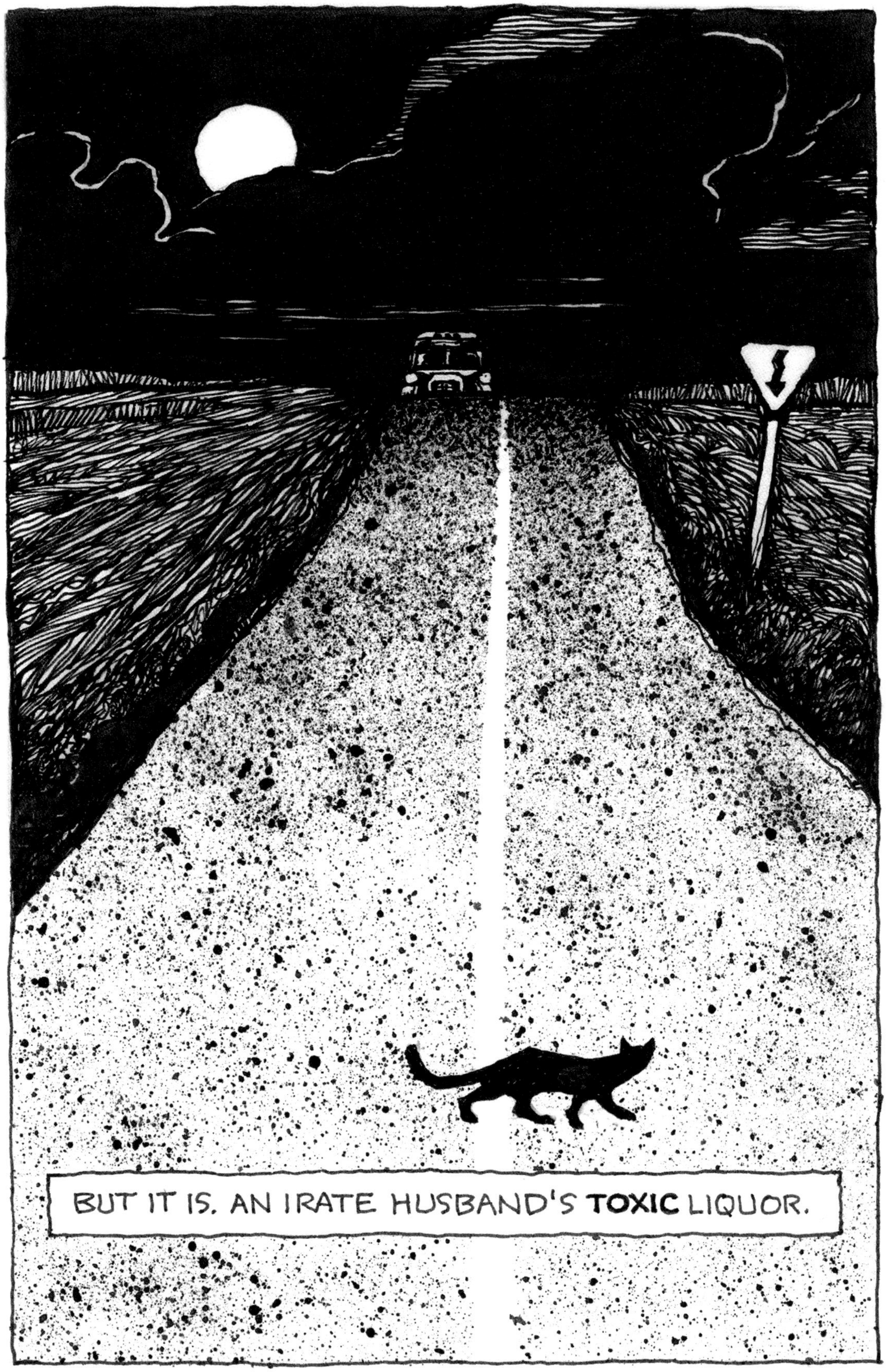
BUT IT IS. AN IRATE HUSBAND'S **TOXIC** LIQUOR.

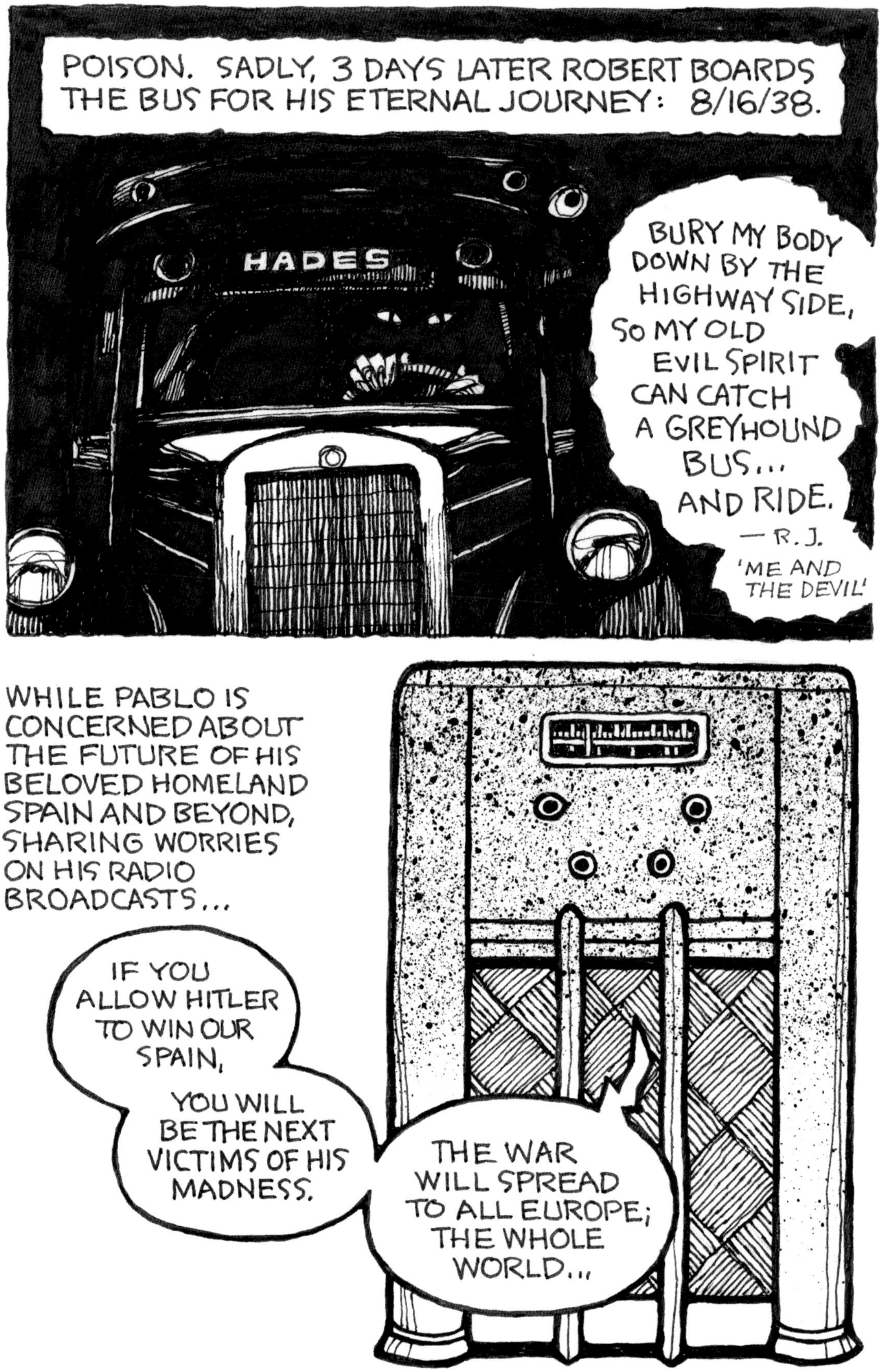
POISON. SADLY, 3 DAYS LATER ROBERT BOARDS THE BUS FOR HIS ETERNAL JOURNEY: 8/16/38.
HADES
BURY MY BODY DOWN BY THE HIGHWAY SIDE, SO MY OLD EVIL SPIRIT CAN CATCH A GREYHOUND BUS... AND RIDE.
— R.J. 'ME AND THE DEVIL'
WHILE PABLO IS CONCERNED ABOUT THE FUTURE OF HIS BELOVED HOMELAND SPAIN AND BEYOND, SHARING WORRIES ON HIS RADIO BROADCASTS...
IF YOU ALLOW HITLER TO WIN OUR SPAIN,
YOU WILL BE THE NEXT VICTIMS OF HIS MADNESS.
THE WAR WILL SPREAD TO ALL EUROPE; THE WHOLE WORLD...

IN AMERICA, ROBERT HAS VANISHED, AN UNMARKED GRAVE IN MISSISSIPPI...

AS A SECOND WORLD WAR IS ON THE HORIZON IN PABLO CASALS' EUROPE.

IN NEW YORK CITY... AT CARNEGIE HALL. LATE 1938, DIRECTOR JOHN HAMMOND IS LOOKING TO RECRUIT ROBERT TO BE PART OF 'AN EVENING OF AMERICAN NEGRO MUSIC' LIVE ONSTAGE IN THE RENOWNED PERFORMING ARTS CENTER. A TRIBUTE TO 'BLUES EMPRESS' BESSIE SMITH, LIKE 'BLUES KING' ROBERT, NOW GONE FOREVER.

THOUGH HIS DEMISE ...MOSTLY UNKNOWN.

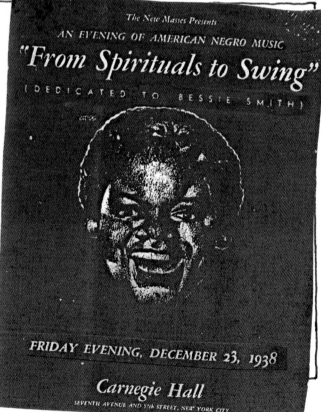

The New Masses Presents

AN EVENING OF AMERICAN NEGRO MUSIC

"From Spirituals to Swing"

(DEDICATED TO BESSIE SMITH)

FRIDAY EVENING, DECEMBER 23, 1938

Carnegie Hall

SEVENTH AVENUE AND 57th STREET, NEW YORK CITY

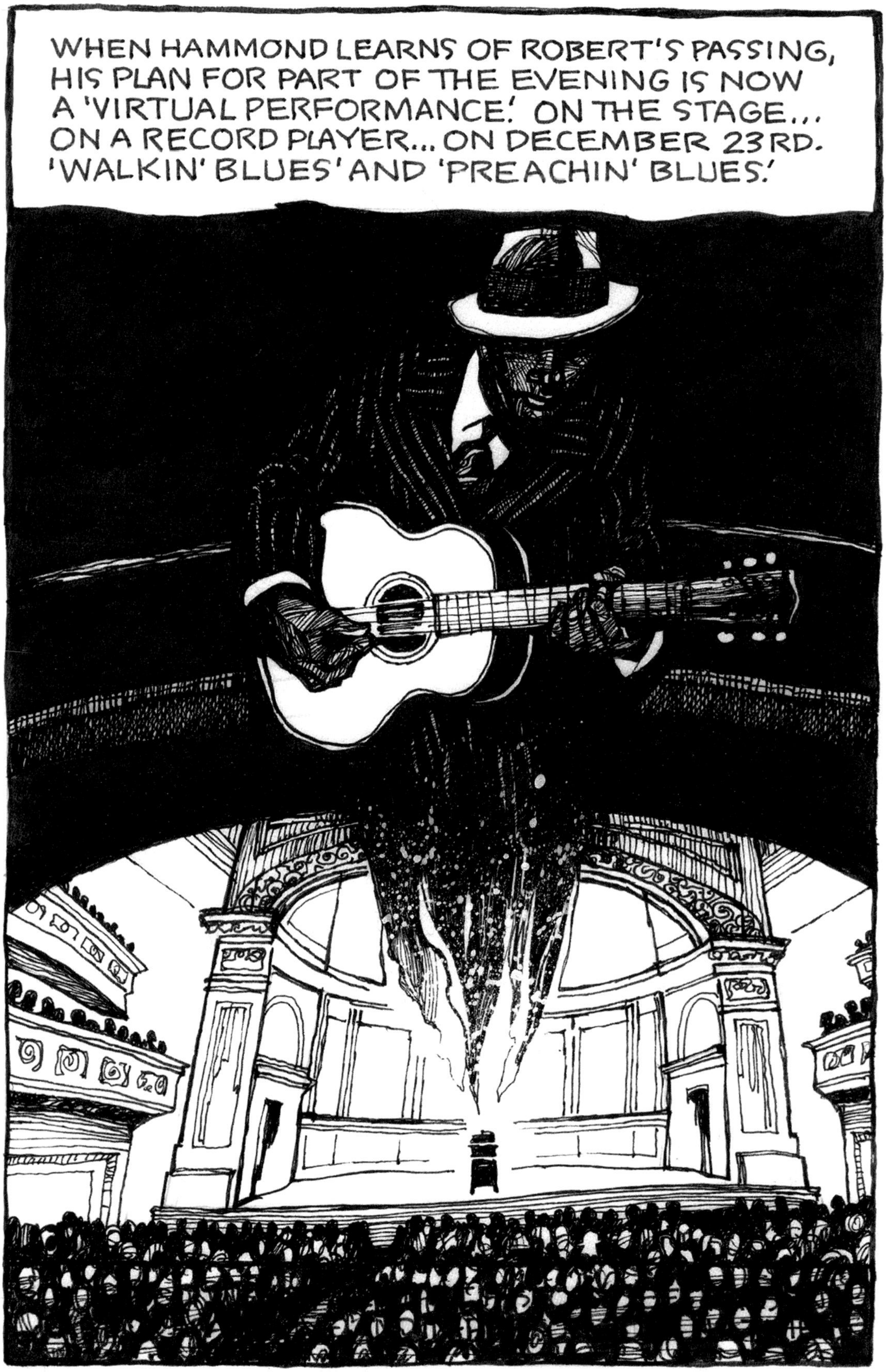
WHEN HAMMOND LEARNS OF ROBERT'S PASSING, HIS PLAN FOR PART OF THE EVENING IS NOW A 'VIRTUAL PERFORMANCE.' ON THE STAGE... ON A RECORD PLAYER... ON DECEMBER 23RD. 'WALKIN' BLUES' AND 'PREACHIN' BLUES.'

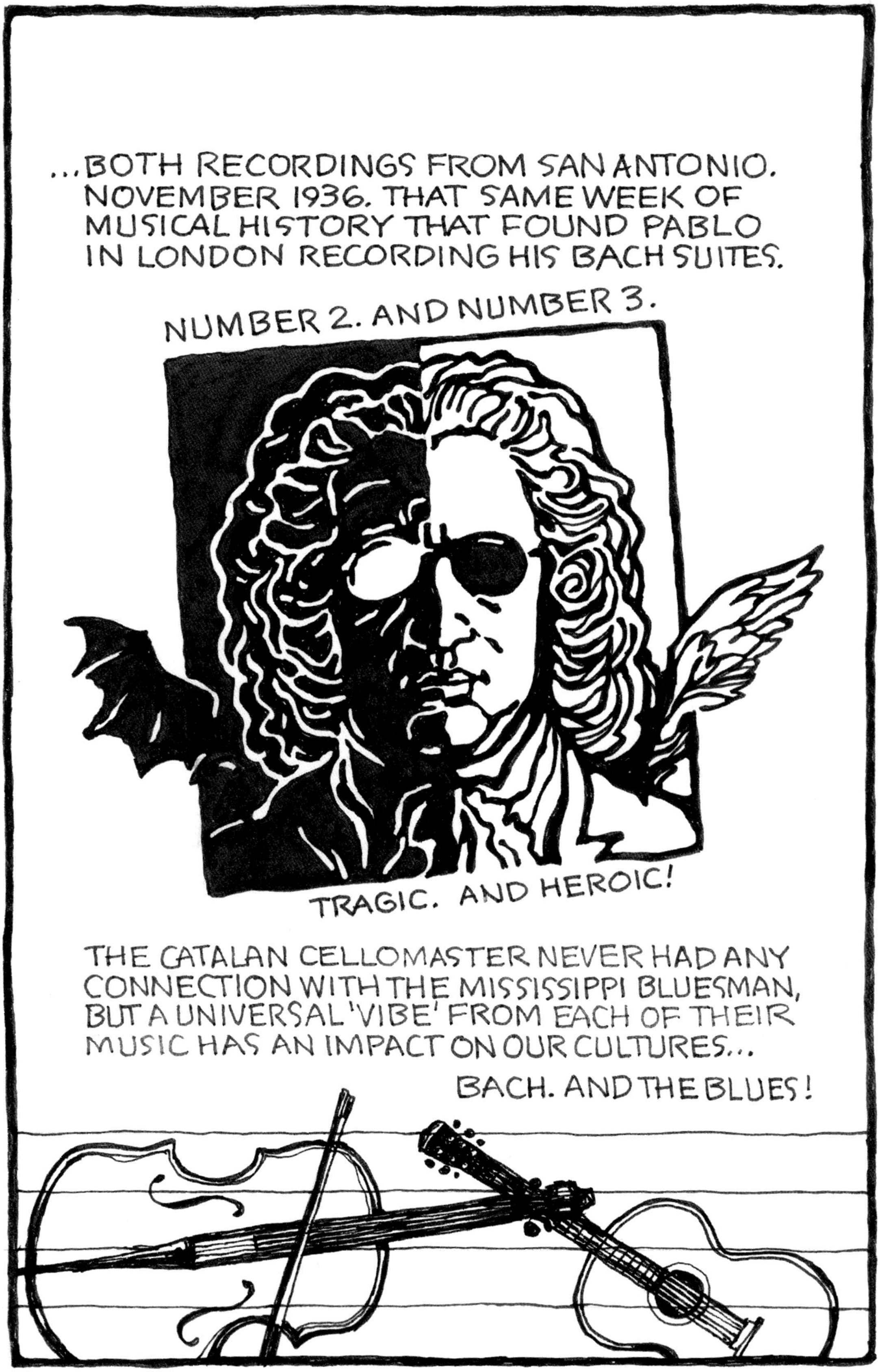
...BOTH RECORDINGS FROM SAN ANTONIO. NOVEMBER 1936. THAT SAME WEEK OF MUSICAL HISTORY THAT FOUND PABLO IN LONDON RECORDING HIS BACH SUITES.
NUMBER 2. AND NUMBER 3.
TRAGIC. AND HEROIC!
THE CATALAN CELLOMASTER NEVER HAD ANY CONNECTION WITH THE MISSISSIPPI BLUESMAN, BUT A UNIVERSAL 'VIBE' FROM EACH OF THEIR MUSIC HAS AN IMPACT ON OUR CULTURES...
BACH. AND THE BLUES!

WHEN ROBERT WAS BORN IN 1911, PABLO WAS 35 YEARS OLD... AND INTO HIS 60's WHEN THE YOUNG BLUES HERO CATCHES THAT GREYHOUND BUS IN 1938. COME LATE 1973, THE CELLOMASTER IS LIVING IN PUERTO RICO, WITH HIS STRINGS AND A YOUNG WIFE, MARTITA. NOW, ALMOST 97, HE TAKES THAT BUS RIDE HIMSELF.

AND JOHANN SEBASTIAN BACH; LONG GONE...

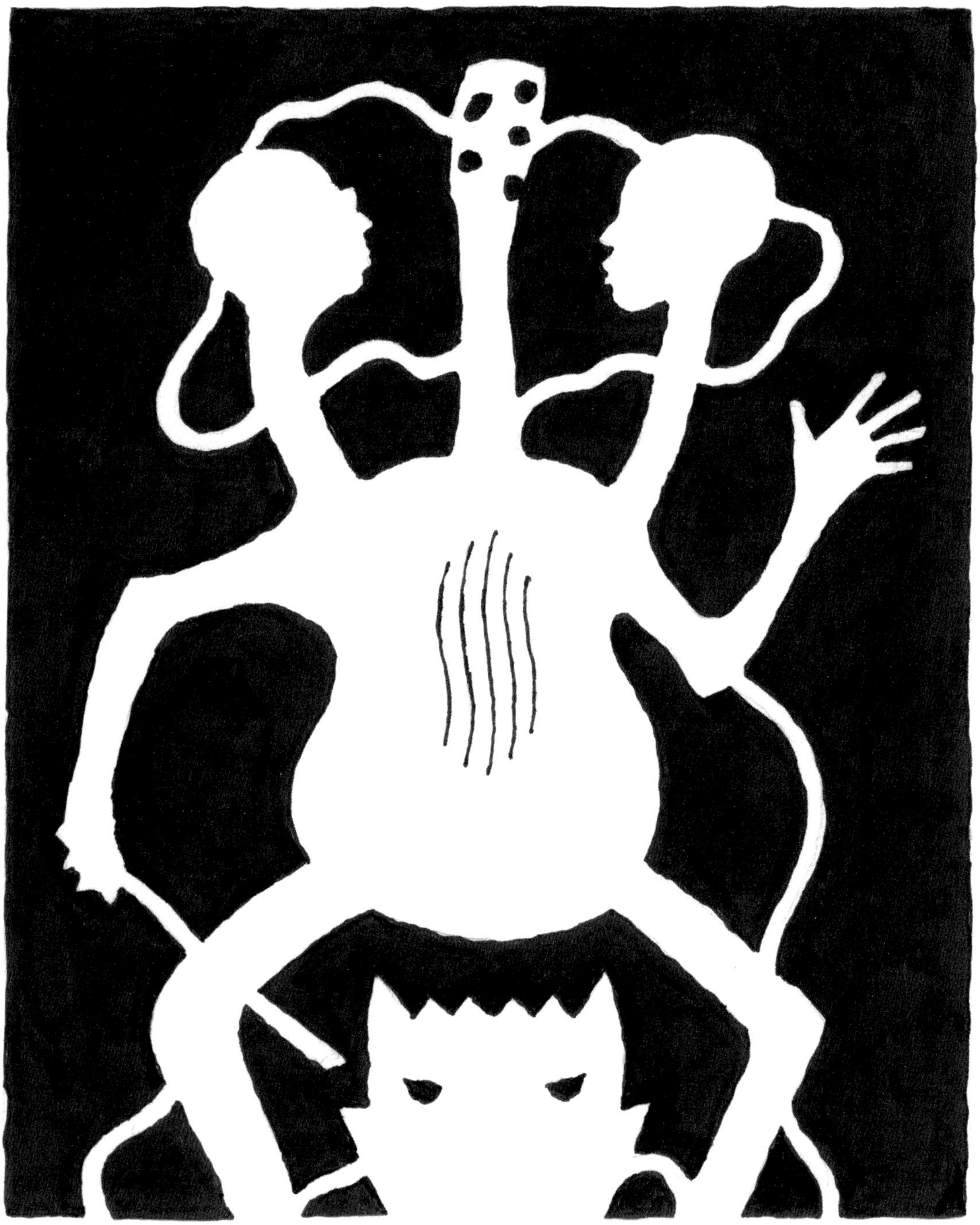

BUT STILL WITH US, THANKS TO HIS CLASSIC SOUNDS.

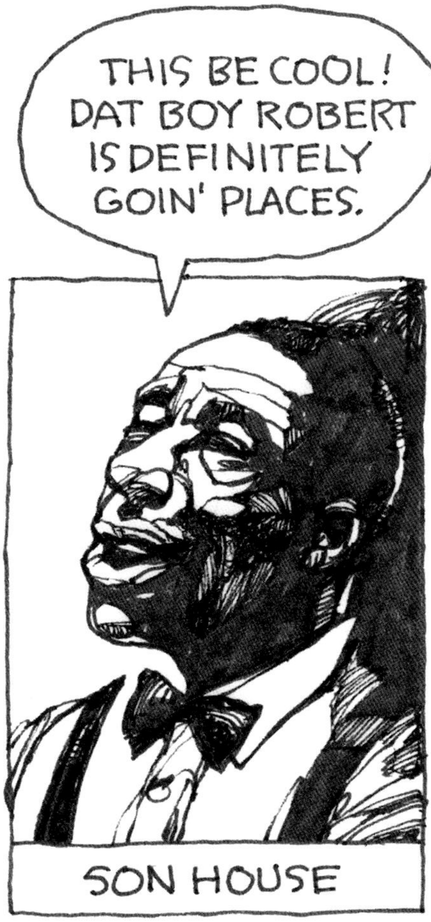
THIS BE COOL! DAT BOY ROBERT IS DEFINITELY GOIN' PLACES.
SON HOUSE

SUITE #1
'OPTIMISTIC'

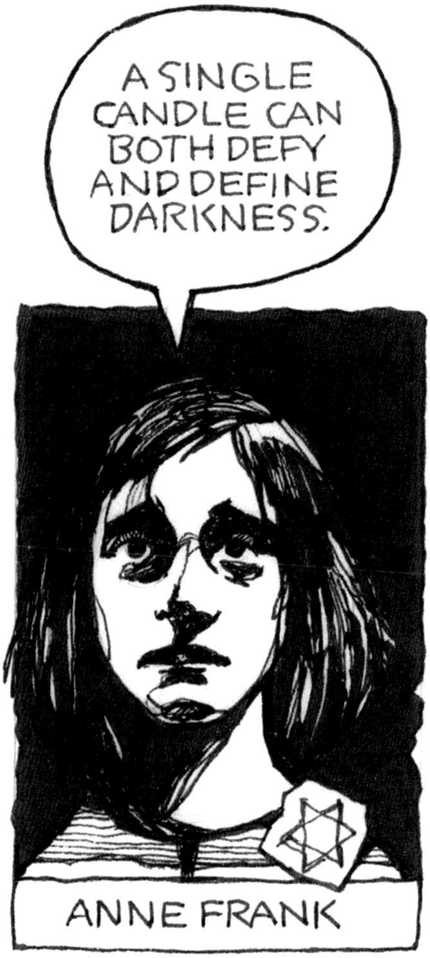
A SINGLE CANDLE CAN BOTH DEFY AND DEFINE DARKNESS.
ANNE FRANK

SUITE #2
'TRAGIC'

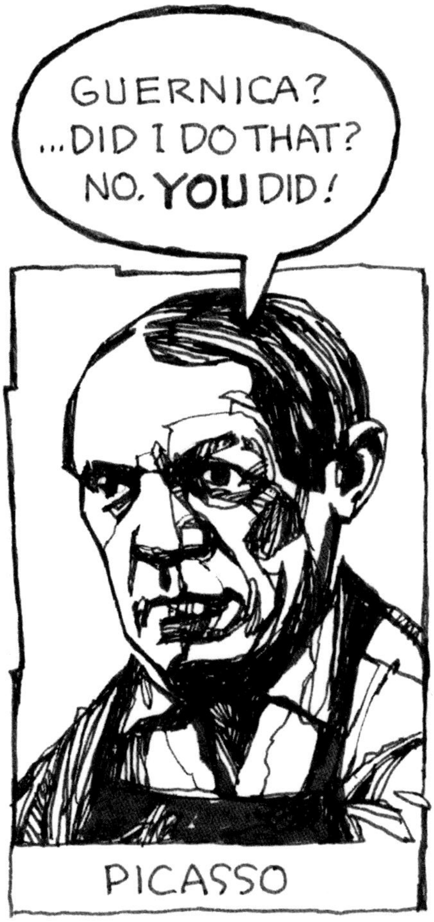
GUERNICA?
...DID I DO THAT?
NO, **YOU** DID!
PICASSO

SUITE # 3
'HEROIC'

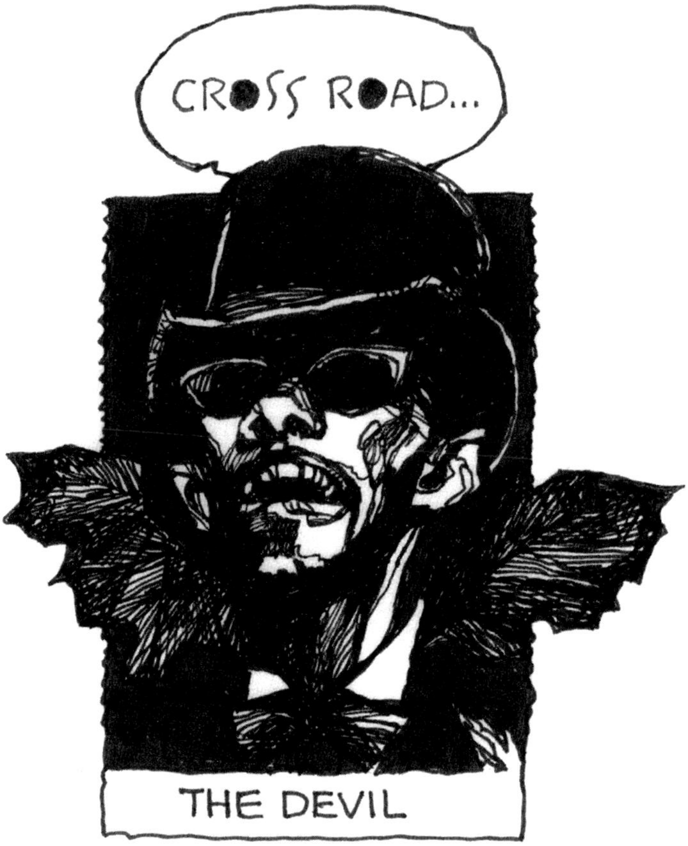
CROSS ROAD...
THE DEVIL

SUITE # 4
'GRANDIOSE'

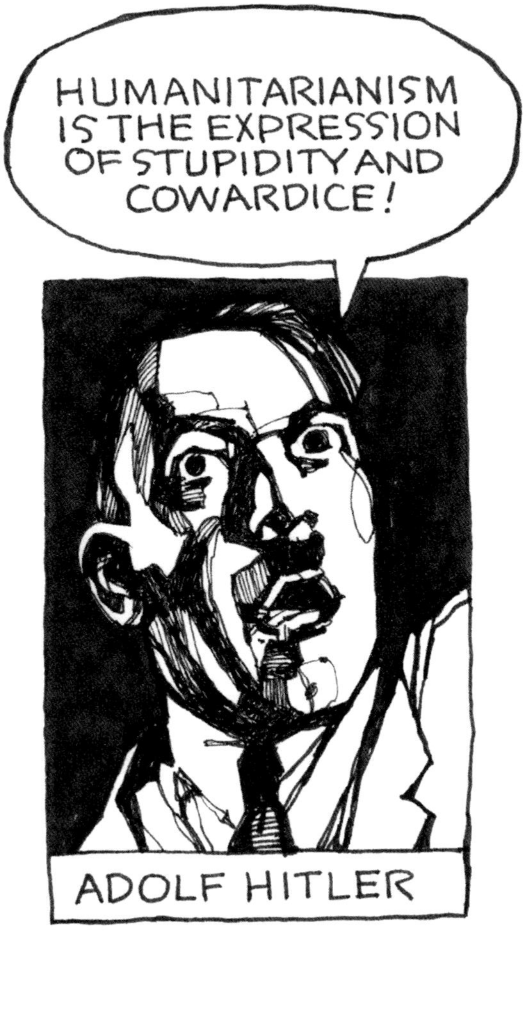
HUMANITARIANISM IS THE EXPRESSION OF STUPIDITY AND COWARDICE!
ADOLF HITLER

SUITE #5
'TEMPESTUOUS'

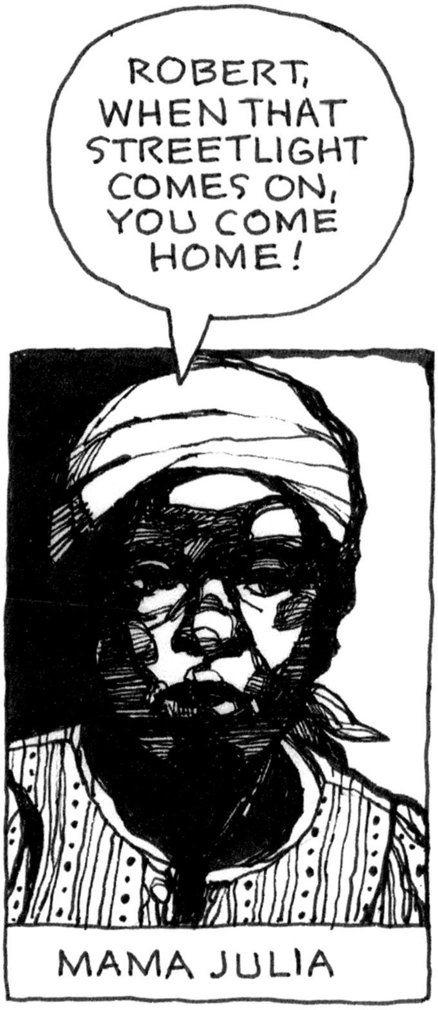
ROBERT, WHEN THAT STREETLIGHT COMES ON, YOU COME HOME!
MAMA JULIA

SUITE #6
'BUCOLIC'

Gary Kelley received his degree in art from the University of Northern Iowa. He began his career as a graphic designer and art director before becoming an illustrator in the mid-1970s. His awards have included 28 gold and silver medals from the Society of Illustrators in New York, also Best-In-Show recognition in New York and Los Angeles Illustrators' Exhibitions. He was elected to the Society of Illustrators (NY) Hall of Fame in 2007. His client list has included *The New Yorker, Rolling Stone, Playboy, The Atlantic, Time, Newsweek, GQ,* the Kentucky Derby, NFL, NBA, MLB, CBS Records, United States Postal Service, Santa Fe Opera, and many major publishers and advertising agencies.

Gary has created a number of murals for Barnes and Noble bookstores across the country and a massive exterior mural for the Google Data Center in Council Bluffs, Iowa. He has also illustrated thirty-plus picture books for publishers in the US and Europe. Including *Black Cat Bone: The Life of Blues Legend Robert Johnson.*

In addition to his professional work, Gary has lectured widely, including the Smithsonian Institute, Society of Illustrators, Disney Animation, San Francisco Academy of Art, Art Institute of Chicago, Ringling School of Art, and Syracuse University, to name just a few.

This is his second graphic novel, the first was *Moon of the Snow Blind—Spirit Lake* (2020) also available through the Ice Cube Press.

The Ice Cube Press began publishing in 1991 to focus on how to live with the natural world and to better understand how people can best live together in the communities they share and inhabit. Using the literary arts to explore life and experiences in the heartland of the United States we have been recognized by a number of well-known writers including: Bill Bradley, Gary Snyder, Gene Logsdon, Wes Jackson, Patricia Hampl, Greg Brown, Jim Harrison, Annie Dillard, Ken Burns, Roz Chast, Jane Hamilton, Daniel Menaker, Kathleen Norris, Janisse Ray, Craig Lesley, Alison Deming, Harriet Lerner, Richard Lynn Stegner, Richard Rhodes, Michael Pollan, David Abram, David Orr, and Barry Lopez. We've published a number of well-known authors including: Mary Swander, Jim Heynen, Mary Pipher, Bill Holm, Connie Mutel, John T. Price, Carol Bly, Marvin Bell, Debra Marquart, Ted Kooser, Stephanie Mills, Bill McKibben, Craig Lesley, Elizabeth McCracken, Derrick Jensen, Dean Bakopoulos, Rick Bass, Linda Hogan, Pam Houston, and Paul Gruchow. Check out Ice Cube Press books on our web site, join our email list, Facebook group, or follow us on Twitter. Visit booksellers, museum shops, or any place you can find good books and support our truly honest to goodness independent publishing projects and discover why we continue striving to "hear the other side."

Ice Cube Press, LLC (Est. 1991)
North Liberty, Iowa, Midwest, USA
Resting above the Silurian and Jordan aquifers
steve@icecubepress.com
Check us out on twitter and facebook
www.icecubepress.com

To Fenna Marie
rocking and swaying to
a groovy, unique
and beautiful
real life sound
your are music
in every way.